THE CLIENT RETENTION MATRIX

THE CLIENT RETENTION MATRIX

A HOW-TO GUIDE FOR GROWING RELATIONSHIPS: PROVEN STRATEGIES TO KEEP CLIENTS LONGER, INCREASE MARGINS, AND GUARANTEE REFERRALS

CHRIS JENNINGS

WINDERMERE
PRESS

THE CLIENT RETENTION MATRIX
A How-To Guide for Growing Relationships: Proven Strategies to
Keep Clients Longer, Increase Margins, and Guarantee Referrals
First Edition

ISBN   978-1-962341-11-0   *Hardcover*
       978-1-962341-10-3   *Paperback*
       978-1-962341-17-2   *Ebook*

To all my clients, teammates, coaches, mentors,
friends, kids, my dear wife Lenna, and God.

Thank you for teaching me every day, and allowing me to share
the lessons with all those who maintain a desire to learn, grow,
and evolve into a slightly better version of ourselves each day.

CONTENTS

INTRODUCTION

In my first book, *Conversations Made Easy*, I shared insights and strategies on how to initiate conversations with potential clients and transform them into paying customers. That book was about opening doors, making connections, and establishing initial business relationships. It was a guide to getting your foot in the door, a crucial first step in any business's journey. That book made a great impact; I continually hear from readers like yourself that they were able to put the methods in the book to good use and transform their sales and client relationship processes.

But winning a client isn't the end of the story. What happens after you've successfully converted prospects into clients? How do you keep them, grow with them, and turn them into long-term partners?

This is why I wrote the book you're reading now, *The Client Retention Matrix*. In this book, I'll focus on the next critical phase after winning new clients: client retention and relationship building over the long term.

Client retention is the art and science of keeping the clients you've worked so hard to acquire and nurturing those relationships to such a depth that they become more than just clients; they become *partners*. In this book, you'll discover how to develop such strong connections with your clients that they not only stay with you for years but also become a source of steady new business through referrals. Imagine a scenario where the constant chase for new clients becomes a thing of the past, where your business grows organically, and you're free to focus on providing exceptional service. This book is about making that scenario a reality.

This book doesn't contain complicated theories or abstract concepts; it's a practical guide filled with straightforward, actionable steps. You'll find ten simple yet powerful systems that form the backbone of the Client Retention Matrix, designed to help you foster and maintain client relationships effectively.

One of the key elements you'll learn is how to handle difficult conversations. Whether it's with clients or your team members, mastering this skill is crucial for maintaining healthy, productive relationships. You'll also delve into the specifics of successful onboarding for new clients and projects, understanding what it truly means to make a great first impression and set the tone for a fruitful long-term relationship.

But it's not just about one-on-one interactions. A significant part of client retention involves creating a company-wide mindset geared towards customer satisfaction and engagement. This book will guide you on how to rally your entire team around this goal, fostering an environment where everyone is motivated to contribute to client success. You'll learn how to set up your "Special Teams"—the customer-facing individuals in your company—for success. Each team member plays a crucial role, and getting this structure right is key to ensuring a consistently high level of customer service.

Referrals can be a game-changer for any business, and my goal with this book is to demystify the process of generating them. Instead of relying on random word-of-mouth, you'll learn how to proactively create a network of referral sources that consistently brings new business your way.

For those needing to get started with client retention processes, or for leaders who feel like they're struggling to keep up, you'll find the Client Retention Matrix Trail Map on our website *chris jenningsgroup.com*, and this book will walk you through setting yourself and each of your team members up with a toolkit. The Trail Map contains practical, easy-to-implement tips and tricks to get you started on your journey toward excellent client retention.

Love the process, and the process will love you back! The Client Retention Matrix creates not just business growth, but also the development of lasting, meaningful relationships with your clients. Your customers won't just be satisfied; they'll be so impressed and well-cared for that they'll never want to leave.

So, are you ready to transform your business and your relationships with your clients? Let's roll.

Head to *chrisjenningsgroup.com*, and open the Resources tab to download your copy of the Trail Map for Client Retention, and use it to take notes as you make your way through the content of this book.

THE CLIENT RETENTION MATRIX

Christine looked exhausted, with large dark circles under her eyes.

"I'm seriously on the verge of quitting," she told me.

It didn't take much encouragement from me for the whole story to come pouring out. "We have a huge project going right now with Big Soda". It should be a great project for us, and it could make my year if it goes well because there is so much additional work there. But we keep running into problems. Some are small, some are big,

THE CLIENT RETENTION MATRIX

but they just won't stop. We can't seem to get one single win with this client."

Christine sighed in frustration, and the look on her face was the one I've seen on the faces of so many business leaders I've worked with: a mix of desperation and resignation.

"At this point," she continued, "if my entire team doesn't quit because the client is raging at them, *I* might quit because I missed my kid's school play again prepping for a last minute 'emergency meeting' with the knuckleheads at Big Soda—all because they weren't getting back to us with the questions we emailed them three weeks ago. It feels like a complete shitshow. I'm super depressed. I can't believe it's going this badly, given all the work that went into winning the project in the first place."

This was not the first time I'd heard a story like Christine's at this company—not to mention almost every company I had worked with. Christine's frustration was just one of dozens of examples throughout my career of this same phenomenon: clients making it difficult, bordering on impossible, to actually get the work done.

But I knew there had to be a better way to approach the problem than simply giving up in frustration (or continuing to miss school plays and sticking it out in misery).

Ironically, when I first started assembling the Client Retention

Matrix, it was due to my own personal incompetence. One of my strengths as a consultant and business coach/trainer was helping people quickly realize that we had some great tools to help their company grow. I had a lot of knowledge in my head about what they could do to improve their sales functions, and while I knew what needed to happen, I didn't consistently provide them with the right roadmap to successfully make the most of the knowledge I offered them. Working with more and more businesses, I began to realize that so many companies were underperforming with clients relative to their potential. It was much more of a universal problem than I had known, and over and over again, it led to unrealized potential with almost every client and a frustrated internal team. There was way too much cleanup *after the fact* versus thoughtful structure and intention *before the fact.*

So, out of total necessity, I created a system to solve that problem. Any company can implement it, and it will lead to happier clients and internal team members, as well as a steady stream of new opportunities that come with low-to-zero cost of sales. I called it the Client Retention Matrix.

The ten simple systems in the Client Retention Matrix are likely to increase your gross profit by five to ten points, reduce your cost of sales, and keep your clients coming back for everything that you offer—while introducing you to at least two new clients per year for perpetuity. Let's roll!

SYSTEM #1: GOLIVE WITH SPECIAL TEAMS

GoLive is a measurement of live dialogue that your team has with your clients and prospects.

That live dialogue could be in the form of a phone call, a job walk, a factory tour, a zoom meeting, a lunch...anything that gets your team having live conversation with clients and prospects.

You'll notice, however, that my list does not include email. Email, texts, LinkedIn, and other digital messaging is a big part of client communication, and that won't change. But it doesn't count towards your measure of GoLive dialogue. At the companies I work with, I typically see an over-reliance on email for both external and internal client communication. Email dialogue and live dialogue are very different experiences. This is especially true when it comes to having hard conversations; it's certainly less scary, but email represents the path of least resistance when we don't want to face someone, and that's not an effective way to resolve a problem. I also hear a lot that email is used because it's hard to schedule a live conversation—but even for the difficult to reach clients who won't use your calendar-scheduling tool, there should be no reason to hide behind email when you really want to have a live conversation. I am here to encourage, cajole, and even pressure you to GoLive as much as possible.

Here's why. Too often, when we send an email to a client, we believe they are reading them all. They're not. Even worse, we think they are reading the email the same way we read it to ourselves. They're not.

If we default to email, we have effectively lost control of the client relationship process, and will have reduced sales, effectiveness, and likely, lower margins.

If you have a client where they email you an RFP (request for proposal) and you email them back a quote, and 90% of the time or more, you win the business, then great, keep doing it! But if you are winning half the time or less, then there is a problem, and you need to GoLive. Please.

How much GoLive time should you be getting with clients? It depends on your role. If you're in a full-time customer-facing role, like Sales or Customer Experience, the number to aim for is four hours per day of GoLive dialogue. Whereas if your role is customer-facing, but you have significant operational responsibilities—roles like Project Manager, Delivery, Installer, Technical Lead—then your GoLive goal is probably closer to one hour per day. No matter what, you have a number. I'll give you some ideas of what your number might be as we revisit the role of the Special Teams players in Chapter Seven. And if you're in sales, it would be a good idea to check out my first book, *Conversations Made Easy: Building Your Playbook for Growing Sales and Connecting with Customers*.

Speaking of **Special Teams**, let's look a bit closer at what those are.

SPECIAL TEAMS

Special Teams players are all the smart hardworking people in your organization that aren't labeled sales or business development, but they do "GoLive" with your customers and your prospects. So if you are a Project Manager, a Field Superintendent, a Technical Expert, an Accounting Person, Customer Support, or a Driver/Installer that talks to customers, either a little or a lot, you are a Special Teams player.

It seems to be a trend these days that business leaders will gather the entire company together and say something like, "We're all in Sales!"

This isn't the inspirational statement they think it is. In fact, most people *not* in Sales hear that and think to themselves, *The hell I am!*

In general, most people have some common perceptions about what it means to be in Sales. Here's a quick word association: Sales = pushy, obnoxious, used cars, high pressure...yuck, yuck, and more yuck. People might also think, *I don't have time to worry about sales...I have plenty to do with my own responsibilities!*

But the intention is in the right place. You *do* want everyone in your organization to be driving client acquisition and retention, even if they never have a sales call or do any prospecting whatsoever. So, how do you create this motivation?

Simple: rebrand Sales. You can call it Client Care, White Glove Treatment, Special Forces, Job Security, Ownership...anything but

Sales. One company I worked with assembled what they called the "Project X" team. It was a subset of some of the most influential Special Teams members that had a high degree of interest in working more closely with customers for both better customer outcomes and better career opportunities in the organization. More on that later.

Let me share an example of a client company I worked with. This was a steel distribution group where we had a consulting engagement with the Sales Team, and we decided to do a project with the drivers. We went to the drivers and asked them to do the following. We suggested that every time we made a delivery, we wanted them to find two people at each location and ask them a question from a list we prepared. Such as:

- How much backlog do you have these days?
- Do you have room to inventory this much product on site?
- Do you heat treat that before you install it?

What we found was that the drivers came back with a *lot* of interesting opportunities. When I say interesting, I mean High Margin opportunities. For example: *You sell a piece of steel through distribution, you might get 20-25% points of gross profit margin on that, if you heat treat it and then sell it through distribution, you could get 50-70% gross margin.*

That's what Special Teams groups are uniquely positioned to do: make useful recommendations to the client that also add profit to the account, and often grow the account well beyond where it would be without them.

Additionally, the Special Teams group has instant credibility when making suggestions because of their role, versus the Sales team that is always having to work harder over long periods of time to earn credibility.

The "Credibility Wall" is very tall, and difficult to climb over for most salespeople, but for the Special Teams players, there is a clear path and it is easily scalable.

Think about it. If you call your cable company, you are probably wary of any offers the sales rep makes on the phone. But if the cable guy comes over to install your system, you probably listen closely to anything they say, and you're probably happy that they take the time to share their opinions, observations, and ideas on how to make your system work better—because they're delivering credible suggestions based on expertise and time in the field.

If you are not carefully orchestrating these conversations by design and with clear purpose and intention, I can promise you that your company is underperforming versus where it could be, and your cost of sales has likely escalated as well.

SYSTEM #2: ONBOARDING NEW CLIENTS, NEW PROJECTS, AND NEW TEAM MEMBERS

Why do clients so often not live up to their potential?

Nine times out of ten, it's because we didn't properly *teach them* how to become a great client and have a great experience.

Here's a recent example from a company I work with. Mike came back from his first meeting with a new client, a Financial Services firm in the Bay Area, thinking he had done a great job with them. He had taken the time to clearly set up his next steps with a well-thought-out plan for improving their team's performance, and they were happily on board.

Within two months, the owner of that firm called wanting to fire Mike and his company.

What went wrong? The client felt they weren't getting enough results quickly enough, and since the market was tightening at the time, they decided to cut back on expenses. Now, maybe you have a phenomenal sales team that can come back in, or a "Customer Win Back" team that can try to change the clients mind, but the damage is done, and it's difficult to wash away the bad taste in their mouth.

How you onboard new clients, projects, and team members sets the tone for what will happen over the life of the relationship. It also establishes limitations—or limitless bounty, depending on how you run things. This means presenting a clearly defined idea of *exactly* what you think should happen prior to the client starting. BTW, if the CEO isn't demanding a top flight, well run OnBoarding Process, there is a real good chance the onboarding will get simplified, and lack of time might lead to shortcuts in the process.

Early Keys to Success

Before you ever have your external onboarding, there needs to be a thorough internal onboarding where you can discuss privately with your Special Teams players the following:

- Every possible bad outcome that could limit the success of the project
- What success looks like in your eyes and the customer's eyes

- Potential expansions of helpful services to offer that might make the work even more profitable
- A game plan of how those bad outcomes will be avoided

Finally, it's crucial to quantify not just the initial value of the client, but their long-term potential value as well. This will help the entire team align on why the assignment matters to the company. It could be a $500 initial order, but it may have the potential to become a $5 million per year account; the initial order size is less important than understanding the lifetime value of the client.

Once you've done this internally, the final step is one that you're probably not doing right now:

Take everything you talked about with your teammates, and put it out on the table in front of your clients. Get them involved in the game plan.

For example, if timelines are unusually tight, tell them! Tell them the consequence of them not doing their part, and the payoff when everyone holds up their end. Great clients aren't just nice people willing to pay; great clients are working hard at being great clients, and no one can do their best work without first setting the client up for success with the right communication on the front end.

Successful Outcomes

Paint a picture of what success looks like and where you ultimately want the client to land. Here's an example.

Say something like this...

You're going to see us working really hard to get to those great outcomes we talked about, and we are doing this for a few different reasons.

I know this is our first project together, and I'm expecting this to go really well. I plan to honor all the promises I have made to you. Hopefully for both of us, this goes so well that you become a believer due to how on top of things we are and how much easier we're making your job. My goal is for you to start thinking, "Wow, I should use these guys on every project we have!"

I know I had my team quote this six ways from Sunday and you compared numbers all over town, but in the future, I'm hoping you just call us and ask us to get it done for you, knowing that we'll treat you fairly, and it's off your plate without any stress. My hope is this ultimately saves you a bunch of time and money because we are so in sync with each other. That the jobs just flow, smooth, on time, and in budget, and anytime something goes the least bit wrong, we tackle it quickly and with minimal extra time and money.

Does that sound remotely like something you would be interested in?

That's where I want this this to go...what do you think?

In these interactions, I also want you to at least *start* the conversation around referrals. Since I have a whole section of the book devoted to receiving more referrals than you do now, I'll keep this brief.

Say something like this...
As we're working together, if you happen to naturally run into people that need the same kind of help that we offer, I wanted to know if you would be at all open to connecting us?

Odds are at least 80 percent that they reply, "Sure, happy to do that."

Your reply? Simply say:

That's great, it means a lot to me when that happens. Out of curiosity, where do you think those people would come from?

Other departments here, places you used to work, business groups you're involved with?

If you just did that simple interaction, I estimate that you'd increase your referrals by 100 percent from where you are today. So why not try it?

SYSTEM #3: COLLECTING CLIENT ORG CHARTS

More often than not, when I ask members of sales teams what the title of the key contact at the client organization is, I get a response like, "I'm not sure what their title is, but I know they're the decision maker."

We all want to earn more business, but often we haven't earned the right to. To me, one of the simple keys to earning the right is to get intimately familiar with all the people who work at the client company. Get to know them as well as their internal team members know them—that's the bar.

Too often, sales team members only have one strong contact at a client company. Even if it's a good account, if that one person leaves, the account could be in real trouble. The person's replacement likely has their own supplier connections, and you're about to be shown the door.

So, my minimum standard for relationships is to have three key department heads at every client company, all of whom would vote for you in a pinch.

This way, even if your strongest contact leaves, you still have two people voting for you. No matter what churn may happen in the future, you'll likely keep the account. And if things especially line up in your favor, the person who left goes to a new company and calls you to say, "Hey, I just landed at XYZ company, and boy do we need your help!"

Cost of sales? Zero, which is my favorite. Length of sales cycle? Immediate, which is also my favorite.

Now, to take it one step further, if you're *really* on top of it, not only did you already reach out to them, but you were also one of the first people to welcome their replacement to the new company.

My favorite question to ask as often as I can is the following: "Is anybody new to the team since we last chatted, and has anybody moved on?"

Keep your org charts full, up to date, and fluid. Get connected to your customers to the level where you have so many people at the client company in your corner, you *can't help* but do tons of work together. Again, you are an extension of their team; you want connection to the extent that they would draw you into their org chart.

CEOs, if you're not asking for the Org Charts of your client companies from your team members, it probably won't happen. This is a great tool that far too many people underutilize.

BOARD OF DIRECTORS			

| | CEO
Kaitlyn Carr | | |

| CPO
Zach Henry | | EXECUTIVE VP
Cassidy Smith | |

HEALTH Maegan Bene	BEAUTY Ryan Richards	FOOD Lisa Burnett	ADMIN & FINANCE Thomas Cyrs
RESEARCH Garrett Perez	RESEARCH Lauren Chamreun	RESEARCH Josh Walker	DEVELOPMENT Conner Medrano
MANUFACTURING Anna Kate	MANUFACTURING Hannah Escajeda	MANUFACTURING Rylee Esau	COMMUNICATION Ian Keough
MARKETING Michael Varughese	MARKETING Jared Cabello	MARKETING Kevin Wilhite	LEGAL Riley Covey
CUSTOMER SERVICE Amanda Welt	CUSTOMER SERVICE Brooke Martinez	CUSTOMER SERVICE Karla Copeland	TRAINING Lori Marino

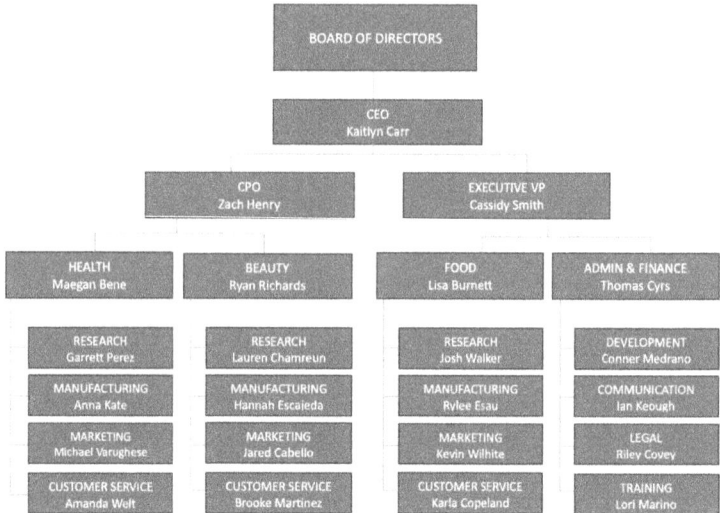

B2C BUSINESSES

If you're in B2C sales, this doesn't apply just to serving corporations; this easily transfers over to serving households and other consumer groups. You'll need to dig into "Who Else Cares" about what you're offering, and it may be more of a family tree than an org chart. Applying this framework to B2C sales will lead to more referrals, and may even give you a unique perspective on how the client is going to use your offering.

For example, if you're a Will and Trust Law firm, accurately drawing up the wishes of your customers may lead to discussions about elderly family members who need care. It may give you an opportunity to refer your strategic partner who runs an in-home Physical

Therapy practice, which will not only impress the heck out of your customer, but it also likely wraps your arms around the customer by them working with other providers that only refer back to you. Another win-win-win.

SYSTEM #4: QUARTERLY BUSINESS REVIEW

Once every 90 days, it makes sense to schedule a formal Quarterly Business Review (QBR) of your performance versus expectations—and the clients' performance versus expectations.

Yes, it's a two-way street. After all, you can't kill it with a client if you're not absolutely in sync. Stop putting your clients on pedestals and treating them like gods to worship. Start treating them like partners, who, if you work together in close collaboration, and both sides do what you say you're going to do, will help you get great outcomes.

Now, depending on how many clients you have, you may have to limit this to a top tier of clients that gets a review every ninety days. Whereas some may be tri-annual or bi-annual. Some might be live in person, some might be a video call, some might be a quicker phone call—no matter how you connect, build this into your process.

Some additional best practices for the QBR are as follows:

- Get them on the calendar early.

- Don't let the clients bail; tell them in your Onboarding how critical this is.
- Experiment with branding; maybe it's an Accountability Audit, maybe a Competitive Insights Check-In. Name it something that is appealing to the client and meaningful to you both.
- Work hard to make the time super valuable for the client.
- Rotate in your leadership team and Special Teams members along with theirs.
- List out any "favors" you have done for them over the past quarter that you're not getting full credit for. Make sure they know the full value you're bringing!

On that last point, it's common that you need to start charging a client for the favors you've been doing. If you need to do this, let them know right away.

Say something like this...

Hey, Bob in your San Antonio office called asking for a digital marketing summary report. It was our first time interacting with him, so we just took care of it. Typically, we charge about $5,000 for each one of those. We're happy to do them, just know we'll be sending an additional invoice next time.

Another way for you to handle this is to give them some ideas or advice on how to do it in-house. That way, it feels like a choice within the client's control to have you continue doing them, rather than a surprise when you send them an invoice.

Ultimately, your goal is to produce a set of KPIs for the client every quarter that alerts them to something important about their business. This will take some work to create, but it needs to get done. See the Toolkit for more ideas.

Let me give you an example: We were working with a Client that specialized in cleaning food production plants across the US.

We could have come to the QBRs highlighting only the cleaning products we were using and the names of the team members we hired along with details of what we were doing for them. Yet, we decided those details had to be minimized, and in some cases eliminated, because at some level, to our customers, those levels of detail were a bit meaningless.

One thing that wasn't meaningless was the amount of Production Hours that the plant was able to run, and the quantity of produce it would move through the plant on any given day.

So what we started to do was produce a report that highlighted the production hours and the number of pallets of produce shipped at the time we were hired and heavily tied their production numbers to our efficiency in giving them their floor back, as well as helping them significantly grow their business.

> **Say something like this...**
> When you hired us, you were down to 14 hours of actual floor production time per day and getting out about 800 pallets of produce per day. Since you hired us 9 months ago we have worked hard to get that number to 15 hours of production time per day and about 900 pallets of produce per day, with a year-end target of getting a full 16 hours of production time and 1,000 pallets per day shipped.
>
> Do you want to see the detail behind this?

You have to highlight meaningful aspects of how your business impacts their business and you will see the results multiply, while your prices increase over time.

I've seen this done so well that no matter how much you charge them, the customer never wants to leave you. You've made them a lot more productive and profitable, and you've made it easy to decide to continue working with you.

Clients are also very interested in their competitors, so keeping them up to date with the market from your perspective—what you are hearing, seeing, and advising—will be especially meaningful to them.

The QBR is *not* a blatant sales call where you show up, ask if everything is okay, and then hit the customer with an awkwardly placed upsell. However, it's fine to offer additional services. I would tee it up like this.

Say something like this...

Hey Shelly, at some point we should talk through what you're doing with heat treating. Not sure that we'll get to it today, but perhaps we calendar some time. I'm wondering about your schedule, and knowing how tight a timeline you have with your customers, I thought it might be worth a deeper dialogue. Thoughts?

Prove to them that you're paying attention to their business, their workload, and their outcomes. You can't help but win.

B2C BUSINESSES

If you're B2C, while some of you may be in a one-time use scenario, you should still at a minimum schedule a formal Post-Project Review. Don't passively rely on a survey you'd send out; actively ask for areas to improve. Ask about things you did that they didn't need. Find out what was most helpful. Keep learning. Keep getting better. Earn those referrals.

SYSTEM #5: UPDATING CUSTOMER GOALS

Odds are high that when you first met the client, you got a good download as to what was important to them and offered some ways to address their issues. That's probably why they became your customer. But over time, odds are also high that things have changed. Critical, subtle bits of information can be lost in translation, or not fully articulated by the client, leading to an erosion of alignment.

It's also easy to get laser focused on tackling the specific problems you work on for your customers, and in doing so, lose sight of the big picture. You will get a fuller understanding of how what you do fits into your customers bigger picture by asking the right questions at the right times.

Also, there's a good chance that the people in the "buying group" who bought the work from you don't communicate as frequently with the people who use the product/service inside your client's company, and again subtle lapses in communication grow from tiny seeds into huge oversights, disconnects, and lost customers.

With every member on the client's team, get updates from them. Regularly ask about their goals, their wish lists, and what really matters to them.

Three Key Areas to Explore

What Are the Company-Wide Goals?

Some updates on automation, different or new markets they want to explore, rising/declining profits, headcount, geography—everything matters here, and it's your job to know this company inside and out. Again, think of yourself as an extension of their team, an entry on their org chart. Read their stock reports. Get to know them even better than they know themselves.

What Are the Department-Wide Goals?

Each group, division, or team is bound to have some initiatives that matter most in their domain. It doesn't matter if the goal isn't directly related to what you do for them; it is critical that you care about the things that they care about. You become more relatable when you appreciate and understand their nuanced dynamics at a complete level. You might even ask to be included in some of their internal operations meetings so you can better understand what their group faces. Not every client is going to grant this level of access, but just the fact that you asked and showed a willingness to participate at a deeper level says a lot about you and the kind of person you are.

Example: Let's say you sell software to companies in the finance sector. This software might be something everyone at the company uses. Imagine you reach out to their hiring team—who didn't buy your software, but they use it—and you ask about their goals for hiring this quarter or year. Then, suppose you share a tip you picked up from another client in a totally different field. I bet showing that kind of interest in their success could really cement your place in their company.

What are their Personal Goals?

Once again, you may not get great answers right away. However, the following will serve as a healthy jumping-off point.

Don't say this...
"I'm interested to learn more about you...what are your likes and dislikes?" This sounds clunky.

Say this instead...
"So, what do you do when you aren't working?"
"Any plans for this year for vacation?"
"What's your family situation? Single, married, kids?"
(Around year-end) "What are your goals for next year? Any lingering New Year's resolutions from this year?"

Really anything goes here. Lean in, ask questions, and get to know them. Maybe you find out about an adult kid still at home that needs a job, and you get their resume and pass it on to another client of yours that is hiring; that could be huge for them. Or you find out they love their alma mater's water polo team, and you discover a website where they can watch the games.

Once, while speaking to a TEC group in Toronto, I had a member share they formalized an internship program for their customers kids. They put them up in a local residence and enrolled them in an eight- to twenty-four-week internship program that focused on a variety of skills circulating through finance, manufacturing, and several customer-facing roles. This often helped their customers train and develop their future employees, as many of them went home to join the family business. The member shared that it not only helped him develop a much closer bond with his customers, who were then forever indebted to him, it also helped him find some good young talent—some of whom later joined his firm. Win, win, win, win!

An unexpected gift at an unexpected time is often the key to specialness in any relationship. I'm not talking about bribes or buying people's affection; I'm talking about taking a genuine interest in the customers you serve, and seeing where you have a unique connection—even if it's as simple as commiserating about the same problems you both encounter.

You could be asking these questions in the QBRs, or you could work them into your more frequent conversations. Put the effort into remembering and creating notes in your CRM to keep you on task.

B2C BUSINESSES

If you're B2C, start thinking about the kind of relationship agreements you want to have with your customers. Maybe this relates to their next project down the road, maybe this relates to expanding the referrals you get, and maybe that referral has a reward attached to it that applies to their next project. In any case, take the time to find out their goals, and file this away for your strategic partner strategy coming up later in the 10 Systems.

SYSTEM #6: CLEAR HANDOFFS

So, where does the sales responsibility end, and where does it become important to notify either Sales or Leadership that something important is brewing at the account?

You can't track everything, but there are typically some clear, high-margin, high-value opportunities that should be put on everybody's radar.

I think of the lead salesperson as the quarterback on the account.

The quarterback's job is to survey the whole field and make best use

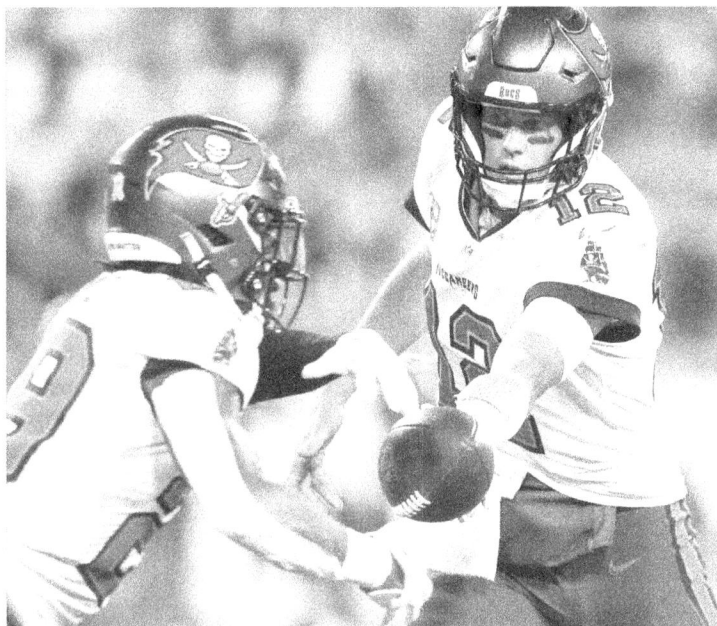

of the resources on the field for the betterment of the team. But it's not the QB's job to do everything—they pass the ball, or hand it off to teammates that have other specialty skills, and let them handle their business.

However, this isn't always how it ends up working. If the roles aren't clearly understood, many people in Sales are rendered ineffective because they are pouring way too much time into running the account and over-managing. It's not necessarily their fault. To me this is a leadership issue: it's imperative for those in charge to clearly spell out who does what, and when.

CASE STUDY

At the steel distribution firm, Sales enlisted the help of the drivers to start to get deeper into their accounts. As I mentioned earlier, all the drivers were coached to regularly ask operations team members questions whenever they made a delivery.

Do you have room to inventory this much product here? led to inventory management programs.

Do you heat treat that before you install it? led to all sorts of service upgrades, adding significant margin to the sales due to the customer more widely using our service offering.

We had to make a decision in advance about the handoff. One choice would have been to have the drivers enter a flag in the system to ask about heat treating whenever we found out that was of interest.

We decided it was asking too much of the drivers' time, so we simplified it and instructed the drivers that anytime they found a heat-treating opportunity all they had to do was acknowledge it with the customer, and text the key person in our office that Customer X needed heat treating on XYZ products.

Meanwhile, they told the customer the following: "Oh, you heat treat that? If you're around today at three, I'll have Nancy in our office call you to set you up for heat treating next time it comes up. Maybe we can save you a step?" The customer was happy, and we recognized the effort from the Special Teams player by a scorecard, public celebration, and rewards based on goals achieved.

> The sales team was super happy, because they knew there was a process installed, understood, and followed that led to bigger account penetration and more commissions. And their time and needless mind clutter were freed up to go out and source new business.

In a perfect world, the sales team finds a new opportunity, turns it over to a very well-run Special Teams group, and goes out to find more new opportunities.

If you don't do this, your cost of sales will go up. Everybody is less efficient. The customers lose out on ways to be efficient, and you make less money. There needs to be a process that is well understood and practiced by all.

SYSTEM #7: DEFINING YOUR IDEAL CLIENT

Take a guess: what percentage of your net profit as an organization tends to come from your top-tier clients?

Most people, including myself, would guess around eighty percent.

Turns out that the average is much higher; it's slightly over 135 percent of your net profit that comes from your top clients. So what does that tell you about your bottom tier clients?

You got it. They are costing you money!

In the beginning with any new business, or sales rep territory, *all* business is good business. You're just trying to get points on the board, see the ball go through the basket.

But over time, the key to a successfully-run business is getting the *right kinds* of clients who love what you do, appreciate what you bring to the table, and are glad to pay your prices, regardless of what you charge. *That* is a good client.

Typically, I like to divide a client base into three groups.

A Clients

These are the top tier. They buy the products and services that you are best at delivering. They use the entire suite of offerings that you bring to the market. They appreciate every effort you make, and they treat your team with respect and kindness.

B Clients

These are essentially training to become A clients, and it is important to set some targets and stick to the rest of the Client Retention Matrix systems to get them there. Remember, it's your job to train new clients to become great clients, because they likely have no idea what you want and expect.

WHEN CLIENTS MISBEHAVE

Often, leadership has no idea when key big customers aren't nice. Clients can be verbally abusive, and it can cause great team members to leave your company. Choosing your team members over your customers is sometimes the smartest thing to do. Setting boundaries with customers in the Onboarding and/or QBRs ensures that you quickly clean up any unacceptable behavior before it gets entrenched as an accepted norm.

C Clients

These clients are a drag on the company morale and profitability, and either need to be coached into B or A clients, or excused entirely and moved on to better options for them.

Once, working with a client out of Texas named Sarah, she shared how she was getting dragged down by problem clients. One after another was either not paying their bills, complaining about the service offerings, or causing several key team members sleepless nights which lead to some of them quitting. Their resignation was the proverbial straw that broke the camel's back; Sarah knew something had to change.

I helped her divide her clients into the three categories—A, B, and C. The A clients were celebrated, and we doubled down on our implementation of the Client Retention Matrix. The B clients were all contacted directly by the CEO, stating that they loved working with them, but that there needed to be some changes in order to continue. I helped the company institute a CRIP (Client Relationship Improvement Program), using our 10 Systems for Client Retention and Expansion. It worked with about eighty percent of that group. The remaining twenty percent became C clients, making the next course of action more clear.

For the C clients, we found new homes for most of them with smaller friendly competitors that would welcome any client, and created a new referral partnership with them so that they would refer us bigger relationships that would be otherwise overwhelming to them. This also worked about eighty percent of the time. (No system is perfect.)

The hard thing to do and the right thing to do are just about always the same thing. So if it seems like a hard conversation to have, lean into it. Your instincts are telling you what to do. If you have a process to follow, it makes it all the easier.

Awhile back, the CEO of a client company of ours, Andy, asked me to sit in on a tough conversation that he needed to have with his biggest client. Due to a variety of circumstances, the volume the client was demanding was huge, but the profit was minimal, and the balance needed to be corrected.

So we got the VP of Ops at the client company on a call.

"Syd, wanted to alert you to something you are probably unaware of," Andy began.

"Thank you, what's going on?" he asked.

Andy continued, "As much as we have enjoyed working with you, we've discovered that even though we do tons of business together, your business has evolved into our lowest profit margin account. And as much as this pains me, if we can't figure something out, we are going to have to walk away from your business."

There was dead silence on the phone for what felt like a very long time. Eventually, Syd spoke with a very apologetic tone. "Andy, I had no idea this was the case. I'm super bummed to hear that, and I want to know what you think we can do to fix it."

He didn't bark at us about how many options he had, or that it was our fault, or that they were leaving or any other fear that Andy had imagined.

Instead, he invited Andy out to their corporate headquarters, where the two of them walked the factory floor together. They worked together to come up with a turnaround plan. Within ninety days, it became the most profitable account the company had.

Work with your clients. Treat them like the actual partners that they are. Figure it out. If you're too close to the situation, get an independent set of eyes on it quickly before bad habits set in. Follow the process. Get *really good* at the process. Fall in love with the process, and watch it love you back!

Remember Sarah? She claimed that defining ideal clients was the best thing that she had ever done for her company, her sanity and her team's morale and loyalty. Pick your battles, then have them. If the conversation seems too tough and overwhelming, keep reading; I've got you.

SYSTEM #8: CHOOSE THE RIGHT CXO

The Client Experience Officer (CXO) is generally a mid- to upper-level manager that is given direct access to customers and direct access to the CEO. Depending on the size of your organization, this might be a full-time role, or it could be a rotational role that different group leaders pass through as a way to balance out their exposure to the client side of the business.

Too often, I have seen salespeople hold too tightly to various client relationships. I'm not saying they shouldn't be close with clients, but I *am* saying that they shouldn't be the only person the client gets access to. I think structuring your organization for maximum client communication, visibility, transparency, best results, and best outcomes are the key.

As I mentioned before, if a salesperson over-manages the relationship and throws themselves too deeply into operations, it can only lesson their ability to GoLive with new client opportunities and help the team win.

The CXO is another key leader that gives the customer a voice. Their job is to think strategically about how to make the relationship more profitable for both parties. Not being in the loop on every prior conversation helps to reduce prejudice and allows for the nurturing of more opportunities.

I have a friend named Payman who took over a fairly large construction group some years back. This guy makes changes faster than any than leader I have ever seen. Within forty-five days, he had a CXO talking to clients. This led to a re-org of how responsibilities were divided up, which opened several doors people didn't even know existed.

You can't overlook the potential importance of a fresh set of eyes looking at problems and bringing fresh ideas. Sometimes it's just a different voice; sometimes it's the customer seeing how important they are to your firm that opens up the doors. Sometimes it's a different communication style that opens up new insights. What really matters is that there are no mysteries regarding client satisfaction, mutual pay off, and how to constantly improve upon what we started. There should be no stones left unturned.

The worst thing that can happen is that you get a "Let's just be friends" email from a client before you even know there was an issue. Look,

I love sales teams. I root for sales teams. However, sometimes Sales is just too optimistic that bad accounts will fix themselves over time, and their rose-colored glasses act as blinders.

In many client companies we work with, the CXO also oversees the implementation of the entire Client Retention Matrix, having the ability to engage whatever resources are necessary to do smart things that continue to engage your customers. This pays off in so many ways, and allows you to charge appropriately without concern of losing customers because of your tremendous attention to the details that matter to them.

SYSTEM #9: CUSTOMER TARGETS, CONTRACT RENEWALS, AND INTRODUCING NEW OFFERINGS

Not all of us have renewable contracts, but all of us have desired sales goals for our clients. The question really is, do we talk about those goals with the person who matters most—the client?

Be it out of fear of coming across to pushy, or a lack of the right process, we often don't. But we owe it to ourselves and our clients to let them know what is expected out of them. Passive aggressive tactics like dropping hints, or expressing disappointment after the fact, only serve to weaken relationships.

So much of this starts in the Onboarding process, which is one of the reasons why I am devoting all of Chapter Four just to Onboarding.

CASE STUDY: CREATING AN IDEAL CLIENT

Jason runs a solid mid-sized company in the Pacific Northwest, catering to a unique set of customers. He noticed that while he cherished his loyal clients, some were just not worth the hassle—they were high-maintenance and low-profit. So, in early 2023, Jason brought us on board to turn those marginal customers into profitable ones. Here was our game plan.

First, we pinned down the Ideal Client Profile to determine what fits best for our team. Next, we updated our clients' goals, which, as it turned out, had evolved just like ours. By syncing their objectives with ours, we were in a good position to revisit and revamp our contracts, setting loftier targets and boosting profitability across the board. Now, Jason and his crew are in high spirits. Even though his clients are investing more, they're reaping greater benefits, feeling more valued, and staying out of reach from competitors. Win, win, win.

If you renew your clients contractually at a specific price, volume, or service offering, here are a few best practices.

- **Do** start the conversation early in the year; the 1st QBR isn't too soon
- **Do** open up the contracts to potentially 18, 36, or even 60-month agreements

- **Do** describe clearly what success looks like for you both
- **Don't** rush to discount for bigger volumes; instead offer additional services
- **Don't** shy away from asking to see their internal rating sheets that evaluate your performance (and that of your competitors!)
- **Don't** give up on doubling, tripling, or quadrupling account volumes if there is a strong business case for doing so, even if it takes you a number of years
- **Don't** grow complacent settling for the scraps when you have earned the right to do more!

Non-Contractual Business Goals works as well sometimes, better than contracted volumes.

Make sure during your onboarding session that you preview the coming attractions of what your mutual futures could look like.

Say something like this...
We really appreciated the vote of confidence when we started working together. I hope you take it the way I'm intending when I tell you I'm looking to earn the right to ask you to work with us exclusively. I don't see that as in any way possible today, but over time, if we got to a point that you wanted to use us for all of

our services, that's the real vote of confidence that I am looking for. Does any of that sound even the least bit appealing to you?

If you are implementing all 10 of the Client Retention Matrix Systems, you can reinforce this in your Quarterly Business Review. You can also bring it up during a project review and when completing any piece of work. Often I see this being an afterthought. Too often, the customer has pigeonholed you into a much narrower relationship than you would like. Be appropriately direct about what you really want from the relationship.

Don't say this...

I could use a hand from you by buying more broadly in our product offering. We do so much more than what you buy from us now, and I really want you to try getting something more each order.

Say this instead...

I know when we started, you came to us for _____. Not sure what your appetite is for _____, but I was wondering if we could spend some time today, or next time we are together, to help me understand some of the other aspects of

your business. If it turns out there is something more
we can do to help, great. If not, at least I get a better
understanding of the big picture here, and perhaps
I can come up with some ideas that make your life
easier. Are you open to having that conversation?

Simple, succinct, and addressing what's important to them, not *you*. They don't care about your other offerings. They care about getting more done, with less headache and better productivity. If you can connect the dots for them in a meaningful way, the rest will fall into place.

SYSTEM #10: GIVING REFERRALS TO YOUR CLIENTS

Referring Business to Your Customers

I consider myself somewhat of an authority on referral business, and I know we all love it when we get referred a new piece of business. Ask yourself: are you focusing on the potential alternative offerings you could bring to your clients, and the kind of reciprocity it might create?

For instance: what kind of business could *you* bring to your clients?

If you're paying attention, you likely have all sorts of relevant ideas about how to help your clients find the kind of work they want. Depending on your knowledge in the marketplace, you might hear of opportunities for them before they do.

I have a client named Kevin who supplies a few types of equipment to the construction industry. Based on his years in the business, and often working directly for contractors as well as sub-contractors, it's not uncommon for him to hear about a piece of business before it goes out to bid. When he does, for his most loyal, and profitable clients, he might just share that info to give them a competitive advantage.

If your client starts to depend on you as a steady, reliable source of business, they are not leaving you, no matter what you charge.

B2C BUSINESSES

Pay close attention to how your customers either earn or spend their money, and look for ways to help them be more financially successful. That could include referring them customers who are also your customers. It could include promoting their business through your business. It could include related cost savings from other vendors or suppliers. If you run a summer camp for kids, perhaps arrange for a hotel package for your clients at a discount. If you manage a chain of pet stores, perhaps find a groomer to be available one day a week. Get creative and look for ways to help your clients save or earn time or money.

Referring Strategic Partners to Your Customers

One of my favorite strategies for getting well known and being useful is to keep an eye out for all the other products and services that you don't offer that your client uses all the time.

One of my early clients, Scott, was famous for this. Scott is a natural connector. He was always looking for what else you needed, and he was quick with an introduction. Scott was regularly brought into deals after years of building up IOUs with clients and others.

Say something like this...

"Rachel, I've been meaning to ask you. Who are some of the other service providers that you depend on for help? I know we've been taking care of your IT installs and network maintenance, but what else is most important to you when it comes to getting outside help?

If they dive in with lots of important service providers, great; if not, give them some ideas.

Say something like this...
Is it hiring, banking advice, legal, cabling, private equity...what resources really matter to you and the success of the business?

As they start mentioning the industries that they depend upon, there are some natural follow-up questions that you should get in the habit of asking.

Say something like this...
Anybody in that group of providers that you think is fantastic at what they do? Anybody in that group that perhaps is not delivering the way you thought they would? I might know somebody better that could help.

With the people they think are great, ask them to introduce you in a simple email:

John, meet Sarah.

I think you're both fantastic, and have helped me a lot. The two of you should connect. Let me know if I can help.

That's it. Then get together with them and compare notes. If there is synergy there, and you both are serving the same kind of clients, fantastic! Make some agreements to meet regularly, get into a cadence, and help each other grow.

If there is a gap in what they need, and they say: "I could really use a good banker. Our line of credit keeps shrinking, and it's limiting our ability to grow."

If you have a good banker, let the customer know that you have a great provider, and promise to connect them. You just built a lot of equity in both of those relationships. If the banker gets a new client, then I promise you, they'll be on the lookout for how they can help you. You will start to get new clients from that banker in return.

Cost of sales: zero. Time investment to get new client: five minutes. Long-term payoff: Limitless!

Be cautious, though; some of your strategic partners will be posers. Meaning, they say all the right things, but never take action. Talk openly to them about your expectations and stay on the same page. If six months to a year down the road there still isn't any action from them, find somebody better suited to work with.

B2C BUSINESSES

There are a million ways to cross-promote other businesses that call on the same customers, and it could be a huge win for you if you focus on what else your customers need. Keep asking them, and find great partners. Concentrate on the complementary service and product providers that naturally would appeal to your customers, team up with them, cross promote constantly, and see how successful you can be, while making your clients giant fans of you and all your partners.

Connecting Your Clients to New Potential Hires

True value add is about offering your clients services and help that you do not charge for. To that end, recall System #3: Collecting Customer Org Charts. One of the benefits of doing so is to help keep track of the comings and goings of great talent.

Great people are aways in demand. If you can help a client find great talent, and at the same time get somebody a job, then once again, you are building a huge amount of trust equity with everyone positively impacted.

A client of mine named Michael shared a story about this. His client was acquired by a much larger company, and the acquiring company decided to lay off everybody who worked in that department. In an instant, Michael lost about six buying clients. He sent them all an email that said, "I'm taking you all out for dinner. The purpose of the dinner is to talk about what each one of you is shooting for with your next career move."

Within weeks, he found jobs for about half the group. Even with the people he wasn't able to place somewhere, he earned the respect, appreciation and lifelong trust equity that we all want from any relationship.

By the way, once those people all started landing at their new companies, who do you think they called to bring in to do work for them? You got it. Michael! Huge wins.

Cost of sales for that new business: zero. Length of sales cycle for that new business: zero. Long-term payoff: Limitless!

If you have been complaining that you don't have time to do it all, then maybe, just maybe, you're going about things the hard way.

If you can commit to and fall in love with this process, the process will fall in love with you and pay dividends well beyond what you can imagine. It's not easy, but it *is* simple. You just need to commit to the process.

Dive deeply into the concept of reciprocity. Be a giver; think of what you can do for your clients, and see how the bounty of implementing and following through with these simple tools can pay off for years to come. Don't measure everything based on the short-term payoff; look at the long-term value of building a highly productive, committed group of A clients, and deeply consider the long-term potential of each one. Ask yourself right now: how many ideal clients do you have today, and what is the total annual revenue from those clients? Set a target for how many clients you wish to manage, and the ideal amount of volume that group could produce for you.

Think big! You just might get there.

BeUSEFUL:
EXTERNAL CUSTOMERS

Samantha, a particularly talented client services director at a company I worked with a few years back, used to have an odd quirk: she had a habit of unwinding after work by venting her anxieties to her cat.

She had plenty of anxieties to vent. She had been asked as a lead director on client projects to help out with business development to try to expand the volume and profitability of some accounts she was overseeing. This request alone caused her all sorts of angst, and she had a good long chat with Fluffy about whether she wanted to stay with the company at all. As a Lead Director on client projects who was primarily focused on operations, expanding the account was outside of her typical wheelhouse; the whole idea seemed so foreign to her. I mean, Client Service was what she was good at, and super comfortable, helping grow the clients, was initially, very stressful for her.

Fortunately, my team was scheduled to come in and start a series of short 45 minute coaching sessions with her and others in her role to make those client conversations a lot easier. Today, Samantha is at a VP level in that organization and no longer vents to her cat about the ask; we showed them ways to talk to customers that led to some great outcomes for everybody.

If you're wondering how your team can make the same journey that Sam made, I'm going to walk you through a framework for conversations that, I promise, will make things a lot easier for conversations with both external customers and internal team members. If you tune in to our next book in the series (this is Book #2)(yes, I am referring to book #3 in this instance), I'll be applying these same concepts to conversations that probably come up in your personal life as well as business.

Let's roll!

B...BEFORE YOU GO

Be Useful...Now

- **Before You Go**

- **E**xpectations

- **U**nique Connections

- **S**et an Agenda

- **E**xplore Their World

- **F**inding Time/$/Resources

- **U**nderstand Who Cares

- **L**et Them Know You

- **N**ext Steps

- **O**nboarding

- **W**hat Else Can We Do/Referrals?

I want you to have a thoughtful pre-call plan that outlines all the key components of the conversations you want to have. Ask yourself the following questions:

- Who needs to be there from their team, and my team?
- Who shouldn't be there?
- What is the physical environment?
- Do we need to bring data to share with the client?
- Is there a conversation that is overdue from being had?
- What's the best outcome we could hope for?
- What's the worst outcome we could imagine?
- What are the 3-5 most important questions we need to ask?
- Have we internally walked through the conversation yet?

I want your organization to develop a creative and consistent way to prep for any customer facing meeting/call so we make the most of everybody's time. Doing this alone will put you way ahead of the other vendors they work with and start to truly set you apart. It will make you more than just a vendor; it will make you the preferred partner.

By the way, I hate the term "just a vendor". If after a year, your customer still looks at you as a vendor, you're not doing this right. Go back to the Client Retention Matrix and fix it. If you can't reconcile it on your own, check out our website *chrisjenningsgroup.com* and come to one of our programs, or get a consult with one of our partners that can help.

Additional preparation includes practicing the conversation with a neutral/disinterested party to drill authenticity. Ask yourself: are you thoroughly prepared with good responses, bad responses, and unanticipated responses?

You can't prep for everything, but you can give some thought and air the potential outcomes out in advance to make the most of the investment of time and energy given.

Last piece here, make sure you share openly with your client the amount and quality of the thoroughness of your planning prior to showing up. It will tell them a lot about you and the kind of person you are, and the kind of company you represent.

E...EXPECTATIONS

Be Useful...Now

- **B**efore You Go

- **Expectations**

- **U**nique Connections

- **S**et an Agenda

- **E**xplore Their World

- **F**inding Time/$/Resources

- **U**nderstand Who Cares

- **Le**t Them Know You

- **N**ext Steps

- **O**nboarding

- **W**hat Else Can We Do/Referrals?

One of life's most interesting phenomena is that try as we might to let go of expectations, the human condition always leads us to create outcomes in our minds that we desire. The problem is, we may become attached to that outcome, at least emotionally; and when it's not working out the way we imagined, we get all twisted inside. We sometimes start pushing too hard for the outcome we wanted without input from others as to what *they* wanted.

Here's what you should expect from any customer meeting. I think it's fair to expect that...

- They will appreciate you investing the time.
- You're perhaps in the best position of anybody to be helpful.
- You belong in the room based on the skills and knowledge you bring to the table.
- You will be respected by the client based on your significant expertise level.

That's probably where the expectations need to end. **What I don't want for you is to get too overly attached to the outcomes.** Stay detached from the outcome. Develop an abundance mentality towards the huge amount of opportunity that perhaps you haven't even addressed yet, and that the big numbers you desire do not have to come from this client. If it does work out, and this client falls in love with you, and wants you to do everything for them, then great, just don't expect it.

Consider this example: Richard has a client, Steve, who over the years has done a lot of work with him. Steve calls Richard with a potentially huge piece of work to look at. Richard stays calm in the process, not putting the cart before the horse, and commits to telling Steve the truth about this job. All the good, bad, and the ugly. He has an abundance mentality, meaning he would like to do the work for Steve, but he's not freaked out if he doesn't get it. He plans to tell Steve everything that could become a problem, long before it becomes a problem, to preserve the relationship, to preserve the trust equity acquired over the years, and make sure the steady stream of opportunities keeps flowing in.

That is a healthy set of expectations. That is the right way to treat a client. Tell them the truth, even when the truth hurts. Make sure this happens in a **GoLive** dialogue versus an email! Delivering bad news in an email is never a good look. We owe more to the people around us than that.

U...UNIQUE CONNECTION

Be Useful...Now

- **B**efore You Go

- **E**xpectations

- **Unique Connections**

- **S**et an Agenda

- **E**xplore Their World

- **F**inding Time/$/Resources

- **U**nderstand Who Cares

- **L**et Them Know You

- **N**ext Steps

- **O**nboarding

- **W**hat Else Can We Do/Referrals?

All human beings possess the ability to connect with other human beings in a unique and honest way. Unfortunately, we don't always take that path. We settle for more commonplace, formal, boring ways to connect. All I want you to do is be honest in the nicest way you can.

So if you're talking to a client, and you know they are headed for some serious change orders in the middle of a project, don't dance around the issue, sugarcoat, or depersonalize it. Instead, own it!

Don't Say this...

"Rachel, so in order to better serve your needs, I think it would be helpful to look at some potential project upgrades that will ultimately serve as great value to you." So polished, so professional...so meaningless. Kind of like how in the Charlie Brown cartoons, the adults all sound like nonsense: *"Womp womp womp..."*

Say this instead...

"Hey Rachel, so this conversation is pretty much going to suck from beginning to end. I've been stressing on how to tell you that you're about to get hit with a bunch of change orders, some might help, but it's definitely going to blow the original budget. If you want to hang up on me, I would understand."

If you're feeling it, they will be feeling it. Find a way to build common ground in the common discomfort that you both feel, and make a unique connection.

Maybe you have been assigned the CXO role and you're trying to figure out how to connect with somebody new that you have never spoken to. Tell them you're feeling awkward; they're probably feeling it too.

Say something like this...

"Hey, this probably seems a bit out of left field. I know you typically work with Joe on our Account Management team, but I figured if we both spent twenty minutes thoughtfully talking about what we do well, and what we don't do well, maybe we can jointly put Joe in a better position to be helpful. If the conversation turns out to be worthless, you can have me banned from the building and I will leave you alone going forward."

As that example shows, you can have some fun with this. I always say that you can say anything to anybody if you say it right. (Hopefully by now you've noticed a hint of tongue-in-cheek humor in this book... if you haven't, one of us doesn't have a very good sense of humor. Maybe it's me. My kids used to tell me I wasn't funny—maybe they were right?)

I'm serious about dropping the formality to your conversations, dropping the corporate speak completely, and just making **Unique Connections** with everybody you meet. Start practicing now. The key to connection is relatability; that's what human beings crave. If you're the most relatable person they work with, you will quickly become their favorite. Who knows, you might even find some new great friends as well! It's not a requirement. But it's a nice side perk!

S...SET AN AGENDA

Be Useful...Now

- **B**efore You Go

- **E**xpectations

- **U**nique Connections

- **Set an Agenda**

- **E**xplore Their World

- **F**inding Time/$/Resources

- **U**nderstand Who Cares

- **L**et Them Know You

- **N**ext Steps

- **O**nboarding

- **W**hat Else Can We Do/Referrals?

Once again, this seems so obvious to many, yet it really does get overlooked all too often. Keep it simple, don't overcomplicate this, but please set an agenda. It could, perhaps *should* in some cases, be sent in writing prior to the meeting. One way or another, make sure you get an agenda out there before you get too deep into the conversation.

Don't make it sound too formal. Don't say this...

"As my valued customer, I'm always interested in preserving the value of your time. So I will be brief and get right to what I want to tell you, and I outlined the following thought-provoking concepts to disseminate."

Say this instead...

"Sarah, I spent some time roughing out some thoughts for our conversation today after getting a download from our ops group about the project we started last week. So, I've got some questions for you to fill in some of the blanks. Also, any open questions you have, let's tackle those, and based on how that goes, I might suggest some alternatives. I could use some really honest feedback from you. OK? Anything I left out of the agenda you can think of?" .

If you did some specific preparation, tell them exactly what you did in advance to prep; that's always going to go over well.

In some cases, the agenda needs to be in writing in advance. Keep it short; perhaps just bullet it into the meeting invite. See example below.

Your Production Line

Send | Required | Sample
Optional
Start time | Fri 9/23/2022 | 10:00 AM | Pacific Time (US & Canad) | All day | Time zones
End time | Fri 9/23/2022 | 11:00 AM | Pacific Time (US & Canad) | Make Recurring
Location | Office

Meeting details:

- Review downtime causes
- Identify equipment issues
- Delivery schedule

E...EXPLORE THEIR WORLD

Be Useful...Now

- **B**efore You Go

- **E**xpectations

- **U**nique Connections

- **S**et an Agenda

- **Explore Their World**

- **F**inding Time/$/Resources

- **U**nderstand Who Cares

- **L**et Them Know You

- **N**ext Steps

- **O**nboarding

- **W**hat Else Can We Do/Referrals?

Do you consider yourself a problem solver? I would bet you do. Who answers "no" to that question, after all?

Mostly that identity probably works well for you. Here's where it may work against you: you're meeting with a client, you have been told about their issues and concerns, so you come in with both problem-solving guns drawn ready to fire off solutions. Your customer keeps fighting you and resisting your solutions, and you leave the meeting exhausted and frustrated because you didn't get to where you wanted to be by the meeting's end. Worse, you blame the client for not understanding what you were saying.

You're wrong there. *You* weren't understanding what they were saying, or wanted to say.

The problem: You didn't ask enough questions to fine tune your solution and have it custom fit their issues. You perhaps, didn't allow them the airspace to vent, or clarify their why & why their issue keeps bubbling to the surface. You forgot to take time to **Explore their World**.

Your job is just to listen. Give them some airtime upfront; only then have you potentially earned the right to share some solutions, assuming they even need them. Sometimes they just need to vent and you don't need to do anything.

I've seen companies give away large discounts to customers who really didn't need or expect them. Is it possible those companies projected their own values onto the situation without recognizing the customers'?

Hopefully by now you and your team have developed some great questions that really force your clients to think differently about the work you do. Keep them on their toes. Take some of the pressure off yourselves by always having to come up with the answers and let your customer come up with some answers.

Now, don't just start asking questions because somebody told you to (not even me). Take an active interest in the questions, topics, and situations that your customers encounter. Get to know them on a much deeper level. You must have a genuine interest in the clients you call on and the communities that you serve. If you don't have a genuine curiosity about the environment that your customers operate in and the topics you cover with them, those conversations become meaningless. If you really don't care about the customers you call on, then get out of your role. Get away from the customers. Maybe consider a different line of work all together.

I think it's difficult to manufacture interest when it isn't there; and your customer will always sense it. Once you have identified some meaty issues to tackle, try to dig even deeper and better understand how those issues affect them, the consequence of living with those issues, and the length of time those issues have existed. I don't care who caused them; I just want you to understand who your customers are, what they are about, before we jump into fixing stuff.

For a more extensive list of questions, check out the first book in this series, *Conversations Made Easy: Building your Playbook for Growing Sales and Connecting with Customers*.

Keep your problem-solving guns in the holster for a bit longer. I want us to do a little more digging.

F...FACT FINDING

Be Useful...Now

- **B**efore You Go

- **E**xpectations

- **U**nique Connections

- **S**et an Agenda

- **E**xplore Their World

- **Finding Time/$/Resources**

- **U**nderstand Who Cares

- **L**et Them Know You

- **N**ext Steps

- **O**nboarding

- **W**hat Else Can We Do/Referrals?

Before we go headlong into solutions, let's assess a few more areas that might impact your suggestions to the customer. There are *three fact finding issues that will impact your ability to help them*:

- **Time**: Clarify what the time investment will be for both parties—you and the customer. If addressing the issue requires a weekly progress report for 30-60 minutes each week, do that. But make sure the client can keep to that schedule before you commit to anything too unrealistic.

- **Funding**: If the right way to fix things adds cost to the solution, explore how they can cover that cost. Maybe they chose a less expensive option in the beginning and are now finding that they shot themselves in the foot by not allowing for more; this may be a great opportunity to increase the spend in the account. If the issue is they need to receive the product quicker, maybe it's time to start charging expediting fees. If it's important to the client, they will find the money. If you're a key **Special Teams** member, please keep in mind that your job is to keep the customer happy, and that them spending more money to be happy might be part of the fix.

- **Resources**: By this I mean resources that are out of your control and the customer's control. For example, an additional city permit required if you're in construction, or a regulatory standard if you're in packaging. For many companies and clients, change is governed, or at least impacted, by various third party authorities; you don't want to get ahead of yourself and commit to something you can't see through. Keep your crystal ball of experience handy and advise accordingly.

Once you've completed this exercise, you're one step closer to offering solutions.

U...UNDERSTAND WHO CARES

Be Useful...Now

- **B**efore You Go

- **E**xpectations

- **U**nique Connections

- **S**et an Agenda

- **E**xplore Their World

- **F**inding Time/$/Resources

- **Understand Who Cares**

- **L**et Them Know You

- **N**ext Steps

- **O**nboarding

- **W**hat Else Can We Do/Referrals?

Whoever it is that you deal with may be thrilled with the solutions you suggest—but before moving forward, make sure you understand the potential unintended consequences and how they could impact everyone involved.

***What* is right is always more important than *who* is right.**

Take the example of a client account manager, Adam, who has a great connection to the CEO of a large customer company. Adam took the CEO and one of his key sales leaders out to lunch. They spent the afternoon trying to talk though why they weren't doing more work together. The CEO conveyed that they were eager to do more work with Adam's company, and the two of them felt like they had struck a real win.

Unfortunately, Adam's team wasn't looped in quickly enough, and over the next few weeks, they consistently rejected the request to bid the additional work that was coming their way because we weren't connecting the dots to everybody involved at the client company. Ideally, they would have asked the CEO of the client company, "So who do we need to loop in to make sure we're all on the same page?"

It's important to make sure everybody in your team is on the same page, completely in sync, and on point with a clear message. Cleaning that up after the fact was a lot more work for Adam's team than getting aligned in advance.

Don't Say This...

"Are you the Decision Maker?" It's offensive, and
incomplete as a data point to boot.

Say This Instead...

"Who else cares about the work we are doing
together?"

"Who else is going to feel left out if we didn't include
them in the discussion?"

"Anyone I may not be aware of who will want to offer
their two cents before we get too far into this?"

Really try to understand all the internal implications of what you're
offering, and how the organization may be impacted, both yours and
theirs.

Get all of that straight, and you're all clear to start to fire away with
ideas, suggestions, and solutions.

L...LET THEM KNOW YOU AND LET THEM KNOW WHAT YOU CAN BRING TO THE TABLE

Be Useful...Now

- **B**efore You Go

- **E**xpectations

- **U**nique Connections

- **S**et an Agenda

- **E**xplore Their World

- **F**inding Time/$/Resources

- **U**nderstand Who Cares

- **Let Them Know You**

- **N**ext Steps

- **O**nboarding

- **W**hat Else Can We Do/Referrals?

Lean in with conviction, with passion, and personalize why you work for your organization. Connect your reasons for working there to your customers' specific issues that were discussed.

Don't overdo it. Keep it to thirty to sixty second passionate sound bites about what the client has going on and how you can address it.

You may need to "Bubble Wrap" your suggestions in case they aren't buying them right away. See the first book in this series, *Conversations Made Easy: Building your Playbook for Growing Sales and Connecting with Customers*, for additional clarification.

Don't say this...

"I've been out there a long time, and you need to do what I say here. This is the only way to fix this. Can I get your approval?" No! This is way too heavy handed.

Say this instead...

"Are you open to a suggestion?" (They'll almost certainly say yes.) "I could be way off base here. But I came to this company to tackle exactly the situation you described to me. Based on your customer lead times, for you to not underperform, I think you might be better off adding the expedite fees and paying for speed. When I think about how little that costs you compared to what you're charging your customer, I think it's your best move. Am I reading that right?

Or you can try this...
"Last month I sat with another customer who shared the exact same story with me. Do you want to know what I told them?" They *will* want to know. "I told them that my production team can turn around this part in three days if we have to. And if they looked at the extra fees attached to the expedite/rush order compared to the money they made keeping the customers they had, it seemed like the right thing to do. Was I wrong to tell them that? What do you think we should do going forward?"

Conviction in *what* is right, no matter *who* is right, and allowing the client room to agree, disagree, or clarify their position, will serve you well.

If this is handled well, and you're in agreement, then keep going. If you hit a wall, you probably need to regroup internally and decide if they can ever be an A client. If not, find a way to ease them off your list and turn your attention back to your other A clients. If they decide to move forward, then you need to be clear about what that means and set very clear expectations on next steps.

N...NEXT STEPS

Be Useful...Now

- **B**efore You Go

- **E**xpectations

- **U**nique Connections

- **S**et an Agenda

- **E**xplore Their World

- **F**inding Time/$/Resources

- **U**nderstand Who Cares

- **L**et Them Know You

- **Next Steps**

- **O**nboarding

- **W**hat Else Can We Do/Referrals?

You've done a lot of work at this point to shore up the relationship, perhaps even setting yourself up as the exclusive supplier in your area of expertise. Now it's time to dot some i's and cross some t's with great Next Steps that leave nothing up to chance or misinterpretation.

I was on a video call recently with a new sales team I've just started working with. This team recently attended a great industry trade show and left with nearly fifty "solid" leads in hand, all with good potential. Since then, they've had several follow up calls, emails sent, sample packages delivered to this group of supposedly interested customers—but not a single sale. What was the problem?

No clear next step was set. Agreeing to call or email someone does not qualify as a solid next step. Be it at a trade show, a warehouse, or just on the phone, you should leave each interaction with any customer with an agreed upon next meeting date and time in both of your calendars—with an agenda of what will be covered! Please leave nothing up to chance. Have you ever bumped into an old friend at Starbucks, and you agree to go out for drinks to catch up...but maybe a month, maybe a year, maybe a decade goes by without it happening? Did you *want* to have drinks with them? You probably did, so why hasn't it happened? Simple. You just never scheduled a solid date and time to do it.

If it's really important, go ahead and schedule the time with your customer. If they don't want to commit to scheduling time to even talk to you, that should suggest something to you. Maybe they are not that interested. Give them an out.

Don't say this...

"I think it would be really valuable to walk through the details of what I just suggested. Would you be willing to commit to our presentation regarding our upgraded ERP platform? I think you will find the time invested extraordinarily valuable. "You might as well add, "Would ya? Please? *Please?*" Come on...it's desperate.

I'm joking, of course, but my point is, it sounds like you're trying too hard to convince them this is a good idea. Relax. Let the game come to you; keep it simple.

Say this instead...

"Cynda, I'm not sure if the upgrade will ultimately be what you want to do, but I'm guessing it's at least worth a follow up discussion, right? (Pause, take your time.) What does your calendar look like the first week of December for a chat?"

It's really that simple. Don't overthink this. Don't push too hard. Just guide them towards your next call and set the date.

Once you get it booked, work to get whoever you need from your team and their team to join. I don't even mind if it gets rescheduled. I just know it beats the hell out of all those annoying follow-up calls and emails flooding their inbox—that's where you really start to look desperate.

There are multiple situations where this scenario might arise:

1. You're making a delivery and the customer asks you about a different product line.
2. You're installing some new software for your customer and they ask you your opinion on a different software.
3. You called them to check on a payment, and they ask about expedite fees.
4. Your CXO stopped by for a site visit, and they identified a gap in the service offerings.
5. The project manager was doing a site visit and they saw a potentially valuable change order.

This list goes on forever. No matter which one you encounter, make sure to book the next step. Again, whether you're in the middle of the sales process or delivery, try to minimize random follow-up and increase the number of solid next steps, *always with a date and time in everybody's calendar.*

O...ONBOARDING NEW CUSTOMERS AND NEW PROJECTS

Be Useful...Now

- **B**efore You Go

- **E**xpectations

- **U**nique Connections

- **S**et an Agenda

- **E**xplore Their World

- **F**inding Time/$/Resources

- **U**nderstand Who Cares

- **L**et Them Know You

- **N**ext Steps

- **Onboarding**

- **W**hat Else Can We Do/Referrals?

You really only get one chance to start the relationship the right way; make the most of that chance.

If there was anything that wasn't made crystal clear during the sales process, it's your job to clarify how to turn the project into a giant win. Take the following story I was told by the CEO of a company I recently worked with: "Frank was leading a project for a new client that he was excited to work with. Many of us have their appliances in our homes, and they were really a perfect fit for our business. The problem was that at the beginning of the project, we never got them to sit still long enough to instruct them as to how to have a successful outcome. So we sped through some initial steps that should have been covered in detail.

"Frank is a nice guy and didn't want to challenge the new customer too much, especially because there was so much potential. The client arrived fifteen minutes late for the Onboarding session, and only half of the people he asked to be there actually attended. Frank never got to communicate some key success factors. As you might already be guessing, within the first month, the client became a raging monster with unrealistic expectations, and the harder we tried to cover our tracks, and do more for the client to please them, the more dictatorial they became. Our team started to hate working with them, and the relationship soured. The next giant project that we could have won went to a competitor, even though we were far better at the work."

Does this sound familiar?

Here's what should be happening in onboarding most new clients, or even new projects with existing clients. Think of this as a chance to train them to become a great client. It's an opportunity to highlight all the unanticipated outcomes, circumstances, and other as yet undiscussed issues, and to get them to give you a pass if they actually happen, because you prepared them for that possibility.

Four Stages of Onboarding

Stage One: Show appreciation, but don't go overboard with thank-yous.

It's perfectly fine to acknowledge your appreciation of them hiring you versus somebody else, but it's likely to work against you if you overdo the thank-yous. Why, you might be asking? After all, shouldn't you always thank your customer? Maybe. However, much of the time, *they* should be thanking *you*. You're about to help them fix a problem and do it in the most efficient and effective way possible, which should be meaningful to you and the new customer.

Don't say this...

"Thank you so much for giving us a chance. I can't tell you how badly I have wanted to work with you. You're a very important and large customer for us." Or even worse "Anything you need, just call, we will get it done for you." It's too much, it may significantly compromise your position with the client, and you might elicit the "predatory" response.

The predatory response is an instinct that takes over when people appear desperate. The other party might now believe that they have power over you, that *will* get abused. Ask yourself: could you accidentally be triggering a lot of the abuse you're receiving from clients?

Siegfried & Roy were a popular act in Las Vegas; they performed an act that included amazing tricks with nearly fifty tigers. These tigers were like family to them. Some of them even slept in their bedroom. (I'm not recommending this, to be clear.) One night at one of their shows, Siegfried tripped and fell on the stage. Instinctively, one of the big cats pounced on him, and before the tiger or the people on the stage could do anything differently, he sustained serious injuries. The longest running show in Vegas ended permanently that night.

Now, you're not training tigers, but your customers can be just as easily triggered, and without thinking turn from a decent human being that likes and respects you to an unpleasant, unrealistic, nightmare client. How you carry yourself matters. Not over thanking them too much matters.

Stage Two: Establish early on who owns the problem.
If you just got hired by a customer, odds are there is a good chance they are deep into a problem that requires an outside expert to handle it for them. Maybe they're losing employees because they don't offer good benefits. Maybe they have a construction project across from a water way with an unpredictable water table, maybe they have an old kitchen that desperately needs to be remodeled.

Whatever the case may be, ask yourself an important question: *Who owns the problem?*

You might answer that question by saying, "Well, we do, if they just hired us." Wrong, I say. Let's look at it objectively. The problem was there before we got there, the customer perhaps caused or worsened the problem by not addressing it in the best way possible in the first place. Just because they hired you to fix the problem, doesn't mean you own the problem—but you will, unless you put a spotlight on the severity and longevity of the problem at the beginning.

It's important to point out to your new customer some of the difficulties that exist in the first place. Overpromising, while tempting, will only lead to problems. If it's a complex issue, it's likely a complex solution with many possible outcomes, modifications, and delays.

Don't Say This...

"Oh, this is easy for us to fix, we do it all the time."

I understand the temptation, but by saying that, you devalue what you bring to the table, and you may have a harder time justifying what you're charging them in the first place.

The smart bet is to re-emphasize the nature and complexity of the problem. Offer reassurance of your process, and better set yourself up for a great outcome by...

Stage Three: Manage their expectations.
Ultimately, managing expectations might be the smartest thing you can do to facilitate a great relationship with your new customer. I know a lot of you are starting to think, "Wow, am I hitting my new customer with too much all at once?"

Here's another story I was told recently:

"Aaron works for a company that we have coached on and off for the last decade or so. I was at their place for a regular sales coaching session we run and we were talking about setting next steps, and onboarding new customers.

Aaron and a couple of his colleagues were all a bit concerned that it was too much too soon. I reminded them that, yes, you must read the situation and determine how much reality your audience can handle at one time, but ultimately, we all agreed that telling people the truth was always the best thing to do. If their new customer lived in an older home in Laguna Beach, and it turned out that there was dry rot in the flooring and support beams under the old tile floor that it was better to remind them now before we get too far into the demolition phase. If we waited until we found it then, we'd have way bigger problems."

Smart bet. Tell them about the possibilities. Reassure them of your ability to handle those tough situations and then go about your business, which leads me to one last piece of unfinished business in the onboarding step.

Stage Four: Ask for referrals.
This always seems like a loaded topic, which strikes me as interesting. We all love getting referred to new customers; we know it's by far and away the best thing for us and our customers. But still, we often don't ask for them. *Why is that?*

Two reasons:

1. We are afraid. Fear. Silly, unrealistic fear.
2. It isn't a play in our playbook!

I think we can agree that those aren't great reasons. Don't worry; I promised in the beginning of this book to make every difficult conversation easier for you, and I fully intend to honor that promise.

I'm going to devote a whole section of the book to this topic. Before we get there, I'm going to give away a secret that I stumbled upon in referral gathering a while ago.

When asking, please never use the word *referral*, or *introduction*. They both sound scary and have a lot of baggage associated with them.

Instead, try using the phrase...

"Connect me." "Maybe you could connect me to folks that you naturally run into that I would probably never come across without your help."

That's it. Simple!

If you read my first book, then you already know the story I'm going to share about a roofer I worked with who was able to buy a residential roofing company and build it up so big and fast that he was able to sell the company inside of three years. His entire marketing and sales campaign revolved around the concept I'm sharing with you, and it sounded like this (please remember that tonality is key. So you can either wait for our audio version of our books, or log into our website for some videos on the subject):

His onboarding meeting was typically with a family, probably held at a kitchen table.

"I thought it would be a good idea to walk you through the project we are starting for you next week to give you an idea of what to expect.

First of all, it's designed as a four-day project. Assuming we don't run into any unexpected weather delays, which would naturally add more time to the schedule. Day 1, it's going to feel like a bit of a war zone around here. We will start by placing a large dumpster in the driveway, and as we start tearing off the old shingles, we'll be discarding of them in the dumpster. Every now again, we miss. If we accidently damage a plant or something, I promise to replace it before we leave the premises. You might end up with some dust, dirt, or debris that makes its way from the attic into the house. So please, if you have a white comforter, or jacket that you don't want to get dirty perhaps wrap them in the plastic we provided for you.

I haven't seen any pets, or cats around here, but they normally don't like loud noises, so please, take some precautions.

By the end of Day 1 my project manager and myself will be up on that roof looking for any dry rot or potential structural damage. This will hopefully be the only time that underlying structure is exposed and accessible. I have to warn you that we find something like that in about one out of four jobs. Typically, it's not extensive damage, and it can be repaired normally for less than $5,000. Remember when I said that since the roof has been leaking on and off for the last couple of years, we talked about this possibility?

By the end of Day 2, I will be back on your roof with my quality control manager making sure that every structural concern has been addressed to code, and make sure that you nip any problems in the bud.

By Day 3 we will have the new shingles on, and on Day 4, I will be back on the roof with my quality control managers personally inspecting every corner, gutter, vent pipe, and flashing to make sure for as long as you live in this house, you'll never worry again if it's raining, or need to call your neighbor to unplug something or put a bucket out. *That's my job.*

Here's your job. While we are up on the roof making sure the project gets completed as planned, I just wondered, if you know any of your neighbors, if you could see if any neighbors you're friendly with might need a project like this as well? I just want to know if you'd be open to that."

Very simple. So let me ask you: what did you notice about what the roofer said in the onboarding meeting? Maybe write down for yourselves some notes right now about some of what he did that applies to you.

This really is so simple once you make it a part of your process. Change orders should be a positive thing that your customers are *glad* you brought to them.

In case the roofer found an extra $1500 worth of dry rot repairs, they got it approved right away, the customers were happy it didn't add time to the schedule, and their likelihood of referring the roofer goes up.

If he hadn't been so thorough in his onboarding, there is a good chance they would have felt like it was a bait and switch and start badmouthing the roofer to all the neighbors.

Own your process, get good at your process, fall in love with your process, and it will love you back.

W...WHAT ELSE CAN WE DO?

Be Useful...Now

- **B**efore You Go

- **E**xpectations

- **U**nique Connections

- **S**et an Agenda

- **E**xplore Their World

- **F**inding Time/$/Resources

- **U**nderstand Who Cares

- **L**et Them Know You

- **N**ext Steps

- **O**nboarding

- **What Else Can We Do/Referrals?**

This question deserves some good answers. Most companies I have worked with, could double in size without ever getting a new customer. The question is: are you sure your customers really know what else you do? Have you and the client paused long enough to make sure it's on their radar in a substantive way?

A client of mine, Rose, sells research services for a consulting firm that also has a huge consulting department. Their revenue may be split between the two groups. She recently mentioned that her fear of bringing up consulting is that perhaps they will be less inclined to use them for research.

At the time of this writing, I'm on my way to run a national sales meeting for a group that, in interviewing them in preparation for the program, I was frequently told they felt like since the customer was already buying certain items from them, that they didn't want to "push the envelope" by asking for more.

Don't say this...

"I would really like to get a shot at your consulting business. Maybe you could let us quote on something?"

Say this instead...

"I know you hired us to get consistent research on what's happening in the market, and I can promise you that your knowledge base is about to grow significantly. I'm guessing there will be times when you still want additional opinions on the opportunities you see, and I want you to call me directly; depending on the opportunity, I can always find the right consultant for you and at least set up an exploratory call, regardless of whether you end up hiring them to tackle the project or not."

It's low key, offers up some thoughtful options, and paves the way for future work.

If you have done that, you have done your job. If you're not sure if it's your job or not, I'm pretty sure it is—or at least we want you to act like it is. I mean to help the client. Sincerely BeUseful and put them in a more advantageous situation than they would have been without you.

The only other "What Else?" I want you to consider is the referral request. I also have a whole additional section on this. Like I mentioned, nobody wants to Google new vendors and trusted partners if they could get a great referral to one.

Don't worry about the results so much. Focus on the process. Become addicted to the process. Get better at the process and let it make you better.

CHAPTER SUMMARY

In this chapter, you learned how to talk to customers in a proactive way that will leave them feeling like you were really looking out for their best interests, not pushing anything on anybody, and also knowing that you were doing your job. As a reminder, here's what BeUseful stands for:

- **Before you go** gets you prepped for the call/meeting.
- **Expectations** gets your mind right going in.
- **Unique Connections** help you find common ground, even if they are hostile, or agitated.
- **Set an agenda** helps you and your client stay on task and complete your key objectives.
- **Explore Their World** gets you asking questions versus rushing to solutions.
- **Fact Finding** gives you key details about their willingness to

commit the time, and money required, as well as any outside approvals that may be required by outside entities.

- **Understanding Who Cares** identifies other people in the client organization that might be influential and affected by any recommendations.
- **Let them know you and what you bring to the table** gives you a chance to assert why you belong there and remind them of why they should be listening to you.
- **Next Steps** reference your obligation to keep things on track by scheduling a next date and time that you, and /or your colleagues will reconvene to complete the discussion you initiated, even if it is just a place holder, set the Next Step always.
- **Onboarding** is your chance to get it right the first time by giving clear direction to your customer about how to win using your products and services.
- **What Else** is the catch-all chance to clean up loose ends, plant the seed for future opportunities and look for referrals to other departments at your client's company and externally to other organizations/households.

If you can make this happen on a regular basis, it's sure to align you with your customers, their other team members, and the rest of your team as well. Who knows, if you enjoy following this process, you may want to evolve into different roles that you formally never imagined growing into.

One way to get great at this communication model is to follow it internally. Every time you have a one on one with a colleague or with your team, it serves as a great model to get you aligned more quickly and minimize miscommunication. You could use it personally if you like as well.

THREE

BeUSEFUL...NOW: INTERNAL TEAM MEMBERS

Talking to customers differently than you talk to everyone else creates a barrier to authentic communication with your audience. If you want to establish trust, you need to be the same person with customers as you are with internal team members—and as authentic with both as you are with your friends.

This isn't the typical way you'd implement Be Useful, but you do want to start thinking about how it can be applied to *all* conversations, not just external. This chapter might be most useful for leaders, but everyone can get great insight out of it. And my third book will be all personal conversations—partner, kids, parents, friends—so here's a little setup for that.

Recently, I was coaching a guy named Sean who worked with a Boston-based company selling a variety of digital marketing strategies to growing companies.

"Sean, you have a good way of communicating with people. I hope you don't change that when you talk to customers," I told him.

He looked confused. "What do you mean by that?"

I continued: "Well, too often, if there is something that someone wants from somebody else, they'll completely change the tone, style, and language of how they normally communicate. It comes across as insincere, and it scares away more customers than it attracts. But you do a good job of avoiding that. You keep it sincere and authentic. Hold on to that."

Not everyone I work with is as naturally good at customer communication as Sean is, and so often, I see people stumble in this area. This chapter introduces a model of communication that will ensure that you treat everyone the same. By practicing this model, it'll become a natural part of how you communicate with people—and will hopefully become how you go about talking all the time. No pretense, ulterior motives, only building trust with everyone, and getting more accomplished quicker.

INTERNAL COMMUNICATION

Picture yourself in an internal department meeting. You run a team of six roofing repair techs/installers that are assembled live, or on a video call. You have identified, as the department head, that jobs are taking longer because the installers are leaving the facility without making sure that they have all the supplies that could potentially help them on any job. This is leading to lower productivity, trips back to the shop, excessive overtime, and upset clients because your company is not hitting promised deadlines.

You can probably see where the BeUseful model could make an impact in this meeting; if the team leader has been nagging the team about making sure the trucks are completely stocked for some time, and now out of anger, frustration, or lack of a better way barks out something like the following" How many times do I need to tell you to stock the trucks" odds are the team gets resentful, feels underappreciated, and perhaps overwhelmed because there are so many unanticipated occurrences out in the field. If by following the BeUseful process the team leader, got buy in from everyone, and had a plan to reinforce the right behavior, and this came up once a year instead of once or twice a month, everybody' life just got a lot easier.

If you're attending the meeting, not running it, and it feels like you aren't getting your money's worth out of the time invested, speak up and offer BeUseful as an alternate model to whatever everyone has typically been doing. More meetings suck. Time invested making your job easier is cool. Let's roll!

B...BEFORE YOU GO

Take some time to jot down your objectives for the call, including how long it should take, where it should be held, what documents or data you want to share, the best medium for communication—in person or on video call, identifying the problem you're wanting to solve for, and why it's important to your audience as well as the company. Will there be distractions to account for? Should phones be on or off? Think through and prepare for as many factors as you can.

E...EXPECTATIONS

Set expectations for the meeting to get your mind right going in. Of course you want everybody to jump on board with your ideas out of the gate. But is that realistic? Will you be okay with hearing their pushback, even if it sounds a bit like an excuse? Have you considered maybe this is your fault? Most leaders that I work with have so much on their plate, that preparing for regularly run meetings can fall far down the priority list, and if we haven't consistently run great motivating, productive meetings, then it might be healthy to consider how much of that do I own. If you can't come to an agreement, how big of a deal is it? Do you have a line in the sand?

In general, if you keep your expectations low, you will always feel happier about the outcome. However, there are cases where keeping you expectations low will not serve you: cases where we are creating liability, putting someone's safety or job at risk, or perhaps a moral issue that can't be ignored. Choose your battles. Is this one of those, and how hard of a fight are you willing to put in?

U...UNIQUE CONNECTIONS

Finding unique connections with your audience will help you find common ground, even if they are hostile or agitated.

Ask yourself: what do you have in common with your audience? Where do you completely see their side of things? What awkward situations exist that will give you power by being the first one to point this out? What else can you anticipate them saying that might help you better understand their perspective?

Being the leader in the room, it's your job to call this out early. It will be a helpful bonding moment between you and your team if you call it out, versus waiting for them to bring it up as an excuse—or even worse, dig their heels in.

Think back to the opening example of the meeting with the six roofing repair installers. If you know that every job is different, and it's impossible to prepare for every scenario that an installer encounters, tell them.

Don't say this...

"I need you guys to be better prepared in the field when you head out. We are having way too many 'returns to shop' this month/this quarter."

Say this instead...

"Hey guys, I know when I was in the field, the worst thing was for me to not have a tool, part, or the field-testing equipment I needed. It always just made me feel that much more behind. This made me want to ask you guys: where/how do you see this issue, and what are some of your best ideas for how we don't drown in this day in and day out?"

This sounds real, relatable, and like you're all working on the issue together, versus you simply telling them what to do.

S...SET AN AGENDA

Setting an agenda before the meeting helps you and your client/team stay on task and complete your key objectives quickly.

Nobody wants to burn time at some boneheaded gathering virtual or live. You will quickly lose the respect and attention of your audience if you do that. So help orient your audience to the task at hand and get everybody on the same page.

Don't say this...

"I need you all to inventory your trucks before you go
out and stop making more work for us in the office, so
I prepared a protocol to teach you." Way too dictatorial
and off-putting.

Say this instead...

"Guys, I need your help figuring some stuff out. We
all know how much it sucks to be buried in a job
and so close to finishing, only to realize that the part
you brought out was defective, and then have to put
everything back in the truck and drive back to the
shop to hopefully find what you need, and then maybe
not even complete the job until the next day. Right?

So here's what I'm suggesting...

Let's ask each other some questions about what is
happening most frequently to get clarity on what we
need to solve for.

Based on that discussion, I would like you all to offer
some ideas on how you would tackle the issue if it
were solely up to you. If that means spending some
money to make this better, ok. If that means bringing in
some of the other special team members to help us ok.

Either way, I want to leave here inside of 30 minutes with a plan that we all feel good about that we can execute for the next 30 days before we reconvene for a debrief.

Sound good to everybody? Did I leave anything out that you want me to know before we start?"

E...EXPLORE THEIR WORLD

This tool gets you asking questions versus rushing to solutions.

As a leader, and as a team member, rushing to judgement and solutions without fully exploring all the circumstances is likely to lead to some half-baked solutions. These solutions will seem workable at the time, but ultimately won't fully address the issue. Remember the unintended consequence! All those times when we rushed to an answer, installed a new idea, or solution, and then 30-90 days into the new way, we realized that we have now created a whole new set of problems that we never anticipated.

The smart investment of time is to take at least five, no more than fifteen, minutes of that thirty-minute session to fully understand the essence of the problem with all its unique qualities. Give everybody a chance to express their thoughts. Give a platform to contradictory opinions. Don't rush through the process, and you are bound to get better outcomes on every issue you address in this manner.

Prep by writing down some of your own questions, and by asking the whole team to come to the session with their own questions written down. Let the process unfold naturally and the quizzing of each other is sure to lead you to the best solutions, not just the quickest solutions.

F…FACT FINDING

Take the time to discover the facts. Fact finding gives you key details about your audience's willingness to commit the time and money required to fix any issue, as well as any outside approvals that may be required by outside entities.

A Client Services Team for an insurance group I worked with was struggling with getting their clients to submit complete applications. Everybody in both Sales and Operations was doubling up on the request and having to go back to the client three to five times per application submitted, which was really bogging down the process. They had an idea about setting some standards that they would fix any application their agents submitted the first time. But after that, they were going to need to hire an additional person to help with the workload. This move was going to bump up payroll by $60k per year and require time to train the new staff, and that extra cost and time needed to be accounted for in the proposal to the owner. By having that information readily available, it was easy for the owner to approve the headcount and allocate a percentage point off the agent's commission if they wanted or needed that help. Being prepared with that analysis, having the facts on hand, made all the difference. The problem got fixed, and we started growing even faster, with everybody doing more business.

This step and the next serve as transitional information gathering that will be key to executing whatever solutions you arrive upon. Is there money required to fix the issue? How much? Where does it need to come from? What time will need to be invested before things improve, and where will that come from? Knowing the answers to these questions ahead of time will aid in speedy progress.

U...UNDERSTANDING WHO CARES

Finally, be sure to identify other people in the organization who might be influential and affected by any recommendations. Figure out who that is before you get too far down the path. In the example of the insurance group, Barry, the owner, needed to know, as well as Claire, the head of client support. Looping key stakeholders in sooner makes a huge difference to get them on your side for implementing whatever you need implemented.

L...LET THEM KNOW YOU AND
WHAT YOU BRING TO THE TABLE

This step gives you a chance to assert why you belong there and remind them of why they should be listening to you.

When you chime in with ideas, make it succinct, to the point, and deliver your points with passion. Don't over-explain. Give them just enough to see what you see and leave it at that. Over-explaining will likely only lead to delays, stalls, and a continued perpetuation of the problem. Illustrate the point with stories that your audience can relate to; and immediately look for feedback. If there is or isn't agreement, and you need to move things forward, move on to the NOW part of our framework or agree that this issue isn't worth solving versus the other competing priorities, and take it off the priority list.

N…NEXT STEPS

If you are moving forward with a solution, you have to see very clear next steps. These next steps reference your obligation to keep things on track by scheduling a next date and time that you and/or your colleagues will reconvene to complete the discussion you initiated. Even if it's just a placeholder, *always* set the Next Step.

If you have come to a conclusion and solution, then ask yourself: what are the things that need to happen to successfully implement that solution? Don't be afraid to highlight what could derail it. In fact, it's better to get the unspoken out in the daylight so that you can address the elephant in the room, even if it's uncomfortable.

If you read my last book or have seen me speak, you may remember this piece of advice:

1. If you feel it, call it out.
2. Call it out nicely.
3. Do it from the perspective of how it impacts your audience, not you.

Don't say this...

"If the purchasing department isn't smart enough to know what to order and they aren't even asking me, and assembling an incomplete kit, then I don't know why this is my problem."

Say this instead...

"Seems like everybody here feels like they have more on their plate than they can get to. I'm concerned that if the purchasing department is feeling too overwhelmed to assemble the kits, and including the most breakable spares in the kit, and they are feeling too rushed to even ask my opinion before they put it on my truck, why wouldn't we just keep repeating the same mistake?"

My point is, there are always rough spots in life to be worked through, and calling out somebody or some dynamic might feel scary, but I firmly believe that you can say anything to anybody if you say it *right*. Lean in. Keep getting better at the hard things. The hard thing to do and the right thing to do are just about always the same.

0...ONBOARDING

This is your chance to get it right the first time by giving clear direction to your customer or team member about how to improve their situation implementing your process.

If it's a new process, and you want your cohort to be successful, then don't skip steps. Just because you understand something inside and out doesn't mean that your audience does. So whatever system you are implementing, please take the time to set everybody else up to look like a hero implementing it.

Think of this as being your one chance at making this work right; you want to leave nothing to chance. Imagine you're about to be going out on leave for a new baby in the family, and that the future of your organization depends on the successful implementation of your concepts. What would you do to ensure success? You won't be taking people's calls in the delivery room, so make sure others are in place who can get it right.

Videotape the process and start to build onboarding content for every system inside your company. Even if you disappeared tomorrow, your company would succeed, and when you reappeared, your stock will have gone up 5000%.

Anticipate the problems, tackle them, get those trucks ready, get the team ready, and roll your new process out with conviction.

W…WHAT ELSE

This is the catch-all chance to clean up loose ends, plant the seed for future opportunities, and look for referrals to other departments that need this to spread the process companywide if appropriate.

First, make sure nothing was left out. If there was, it becomes an agenda item on the next step that you set.

Second, ask yourself, "Is there any place else in our organization that this concept would apply? Is there another group that needs this?"

Third, look for referrals to current and past clients that could be helped by getting an update on your internal process, and decide which team member is best suited to contact the customer with this information.

It should only take around thirty minutes for you and the whole team to feel good about the discussion. Your team efficiently made some great progress, and everyone's life was made easier. For that, you should smile and feel good about the impact you are having on your internal and external customers. After that, rinse and repeat! Make this process a habit that works for you. Teach this habit to others. Live in the solution and get really good at efficiently addressing problems.

## FOUR

SUCCESSFUL ONBOARDING OF NEW PROJECTS AND CUSTOMERS

The older I get, the more I appreciate the mistakes I've made, and how I can use those mistakes to good purpose. Some mistakes I only witnessed—some, I had to make myself to fully appreciate their significance.

I was recently talking to the former CEO of a large engineering services company who had just sat in on my program regarding the material you're about to learn in this chapter.

He said, "We used to win these great big projects that could have been super profitable and would have led to all sorts of follow on work down the road at some really high margins. But, invariably, the people who bought the services were very different from the people who *used* the services. Once we got a contract signed and finished celebrating the big win, we got dragged down in the muck, because not all of the people we had to work with every day were invited to the table to weigh in with their thoughts, and they already had relationships formed with other service providers.

So rather than help us get a win at every project, they were often hoping we would fail. Sometimes they'd even *cause* us to fail out of some twisted loyalty to the former supplier that was giving them Steelers Tickets, or some other veiled form of bribery.

I really wish I had seen your system years ago."

I'm guessing that the majority of you reading this already believe that your company has a good onboarding process for new clients and projects. And you probably do.

My question is really about the consistent execution of that process. If there were two to four subtle improvements that could be made, could you turn that customer from a good volume of $1M per year, to an incredible $4M per year?

Don't underestimate the significance of getting a new customer started, and the impact it can make.

Pete Carol, coach of the Seattle Seahawks, shared a story about his commitment to onboarding new players. At one point, he had the best record in the NFL for undrafted rookies having successful careers at the highest level.

He was talking to a mentor of his that was an Admiral in charge of training the Special Forces units, and they were having a really hard time with people graduating from the program. They would pick the top of the top people coming out of the naval academy, and finding that only 1 out of 3 made it through their program. This was obviously expensive and demoralizing on all sorts of levels.

They decided to assign a mentor to each participant in the training program, who was a former graduate, just to study and identify what the problem was. What they found was that without adjusting the training program at all, they immediately increased the graduation rate to 2 out of 3, just because they had paid closer attention to each one of the participants by assigning a mentor.

So I want you to start to think of the possibility of increasing the results you get out of each client, and doubling your double. It's going to take some work, but the payoff will be tremendous.

CASE STUDY: A BOTCHED ONBOARDING

Trever was pretty stoked the day they received their first PO from a large, household-name specialty aerospace/technology company. The potential was sky-high in more ways than one. Although their initial orders started at hundreds to thousands of dollars per week, we all knew this could become their marquee client, billing hundreds of thousands of dollars PER WEEK!

Unfortunately, this is now serving as the "What not to do" example in this book. Here's what happened: Trever received a call from 'The Big Prospect' saying they were having problems with their current supplier and that they wanted to talk with him about helping them out. Trever and his team quickly got in front of the group within this behemoth of a company, got on the AVL (approved vendor list), and they started ordering almost immediately. In an effort to be "accommodating" to their new, big customer, they did not want to "slow down" their buying process and quickly started fulfilling orders.

The problem was this: That group that called Trever's company only represented a very small portion of the overall business and had little pull when it came to larger corporate decisions.

In the rush of getting them on board, we didn't zero in on the larger problem they were experiencing with late orders. We didn't get an org chart, we didn't get to know any of the other buyers/decision-makers, and their competitors had relationships at much higher and deeper levels. When they realized they had lost that portion of the business to Trever's company, they leveraged those higher-level relationships to undo the relationship with Trever's company. What could have—and should have—become a great marquee, multi-million-dollar-per-year piece of business, quickly devolved into a few orders over a few months, and they lost the business as quickly as they had gained it.

In debriefing what happened with Trever after the fact, he is lamenting the missed opportunity but is using this as an important lesson to insist on proper, thorough, and timely onboarding with every client, every time. Sometimes the most painful lessons have the most lasting and impactful positive effects over the long haul.

I have always said you can learn from your own mistakes or somebody else's. Learning from others is far less costly and far less gut-wrenching for the person learning the lesson.

Earlier in this book I laid out my four-step process regarding successful onboarding:

1. Appreciation without going overboard on thank-yous.
2. Acknowledgement of the existing problem and what it will take to correct it.
3. Managing expectations about all the potential unknowns that could surface.
4. Planting the seed for additional business & receiving referrals.

If you want a model to follow for on boarding, I am going to use the rest of this section to walk you through our template and process to make this easy to implement inside your organization.

In fact, if you go to *chrisjenningsgroup.com* you can download our onboarding template now and make notes on it as you read this.

CHRIS
JENNINGS
GROUP
SALES LEADERSHIP & CLIENT RETENTION

10 Step Onboarding Template

1. Appreciation & Acknowledgement.

2. Acknowledge how big of a problem they have and don't be afraid to remind them of the complexity associated with solving their problem. Yes, their problem.

3. Start training your client how to become a great client right away.

4. Talk internally first about the new customer, or new project, before talking to the customer in depth.

5. Establish the cadence to your kickoff process and get it on the calendar.

6. External kick off meeting number #1.

7. Manage the Expectations.

8. Ask what a win looks like for them.

9. Paint the picture of what the future could look like.

10. Referrals & getting doors opened for you that would stay otherwise closed, or unknown.

Remember my story of the roofer and the excellent job he did, and what it did for his business? (If not, see Chapter Two.)

I was running an annual sales meeting for a friend and client named Mark yesterday. He runs a good size privately held company out of New Jersey. One of the big focusses for his company was improving their onboarding process for new projects with existing clients, and ramping up the coordinated effort of the special teams group to better manage and strengthen those relationships with the ultimate goal of doing more business with each client.

He shared how he had just switched banks to one that was more business-oriented. Mark is the ideal client that they probably want to hold onto forever—grow with him, and do lots of easy business with a much lower cost of sales now that they have acquired him as a new client.

Mark said he was struck by the time and attention to detail that his new banker provided. Not only his primary contact, but a team of about five people are included on each weekly call to help facilitate the transition and minimize the number of headaches in making the switch.

While not knowing them very long, he's already convinced he made a great choice. He's talking them up to every interested person he meets. He's investing his limited available time resource into establishing this new relationship, which will reduce the likelihood of him wanting to invest more time in any alternate banking options. Life is hard, and any business partner that can make things a little easier is worth its weight in gold.

I can guarantee you this. The odds of Mark giving all of his business for the rest of his time on this planet, and regularly referring everybody he encounters to this bank went up five-fold!

Don't think of the value of the single purchase that your customer just made. Think of the lifetime value of every new client you work with if they were to purchase everything you offer for as long as you both were in business.

The value of Mark's business to this bank in Year 1 may only net a profit of $10,000-$25,000 dollars. However, the lifetime value of Mark's business could easily be well over $1 million to $3 million in net profit. So, if you aren't motivated to hold onto the clients like Mark because of the smaller profits you initially receive from them, think again. It's not only Mark's lifetime value to his bank; let's pretend that Mark refers ten people over the course of the next ten years. If the bank continues with their excellent onboarding process, they can count on adding another $10 million-$30 million in future net profits from acquiring this one customer and onboarding them the right way.

If you like the following, download our "Client Lifetime Value Calculator" at *chrisjenningsgroup.com*.

Name of Client	Current Services Provided	Initial Order Size	Current Average Annual Revenue	Potential Services they could buy	Potential Annual Revenue	Number of years they could be a client	Lifetime Value of the Clients	Unrealized Revenue From Existing Clients
Note to reader: The Calculator Should give you an ongoing potential upside number to be displayed for the entire company as an aggregate number								
The Jones Co.	Shipping	$350	$2150/year	Packing/logistic planning/overseas	$240,000/year	20 years	$4,800,000	$4,798,850
Clairmont University	Shipping	$175	$1800/year	Logistics Planning/Vendor Management/Student Book Delivery	$110,000/year	25 years	$2,750,000	$2,748,000
							Total=	7,546,850

Make this calculator public for entire company. Bonus where appropriate

Now are you thinking this is worth digging into? I know we are all busy. I said this before, **the hard thing to do and the right thing to do are usually the same.** If it's harder for you to roll out the red carpet in a thoughtful way, and get your whole special teams group assembled to get your clients started on the right foot. Well, there's a good reason why.

It's possible that your best salesperson actually *isn't* the best person to orchestrate this effort. In fact, that person may need to come from the **Special Teams!**

I look at great salespeople like great quarterbacks. The quarterback's job is to survey the field, and make best use of the resources around them. They rarely are the one crossing the goal line, and they never get there without significant help from their team.

So salespeople are much better suited to go out and find great customers, put the special teams players in the best position to do what they do well, and then get busy and go find another great customer. Rinse and repeat. Get good at the process. Fall in love with the process, and let the process love you back.

10 STEP ONBOARDING TEMPLATE

1. Appreciation & Acknowledgement

Develop a phrase that rings true for you and your team about what it means to you when a client hires you or expands their business with you versus the number of other options they had.

Don't say this...

"Thank you so much for giving us a shot," or "It means the world to me to be able to work with you," or "We can't thank you enough for trusting us with your accounts."

To me, all of these are a bit over the top, and sound like we are trying too hard, or a little desperate, or even worse, incompetent and unworthy of their trust.

Say this instead....

"Mark, I appreciate the vote of confidence," or "It matters to me that you chose us over your other options," or "We both went through some real soul searching to get here & I hope your feeling as good about where we landed and as confident as I am on where this could lead?"

These are all more understated, acknowledging their choice, reaffirming of the choice, but not going overboard. Honestly, they really should be thanking you for taking them on as a client. I mean that. Yes they are paying you. Yes, they could have gone elsewhere, but you are the one who is about to do a bunch of work for them, and you are the one that is going to show them the way to the promise land of whatever that looks like when you get them rolling. Please don't ever put yourself in a sub-servient role to your customer. All customers are really partners. As partners, they have some responsibilities, we have some responsibilities, to get the best outcomes, we both need to contribute some real blood, sweat, and yes, tears.

2. **Acknowledge how big of a problem they have and don't be afraid to remind them of the complexity associated with solving their problem. Yes, *their* problem.**

Odds are they have been struggling with late shipments, poor management structure, inadequate cash flow, limited IT resources, or whatever their issue is for a long time. You may have to point out the complexity, especially if it's a new problem. If you don't do this early, they may not fully appreciate the effort you are about to poor into this. Don't freak out at my suggestion—just tell them the truth. Say it nicely. Don't over exaggerate, or under exaggerate. Most of all, please don't over-promise, and under-deliver. Lots of us in sales like to promise a rosy future, but the reality is, there will be a thorny start to the project, and not all problems get fixed right away.

If you don't do this early enough, you run the risk of them putting undue pressure on you to fix stuff. They might try to bully you into some scope creep, you'll get resentful towards them, start doing things for them for free, not getting credit for it even, and ultimately, you won't have that great lifelong relationship you were hoping would develop.

3. Start training your client how to become a great client right away.

Imagine that you bring a new puppy home, and because she is so cute, you let her sleep alongside you in your bed for the first week. She's a puppy, so of course she soils your sheets. You tell her "It's okay!" in a singsong voice, and still let her sleep in the bed with you. Well guess what, once the cuteness wears off, and you try to get her out of your bed and into a crate, or her own dog bed, it may be too late. You get one chance to train a puppy the right way. You often only get one chance to train a client how to be a great client. Start early. Night one, in the crate! She will be happier in the long run, and so will you.

As soon as the client says yes, signs your agreement, and you've issued a PO, and/or cut your first check, immediately start to walk them through the process of what is ahead of them. You have been through this thousands of times, but this may be their first time. They may have preconceived notions of how this works, which are completely contrary to what you need from them for a successful outcome. They may feel that their work is done, and are eagerly pushing everything to you, and they need to be an active participant in the solution. The clock and calendar move so fast, that precious time gets squandered due to a variety of vacation, holiday, weather, and other logistical delays that could have them frustrated with the lack of progress if you aren't monitoring the clock and keeping everybody on point.

Reference your Ideal Client worksheet, and start training them to move in that direction on Day 1—even better, make it a part of the sales process.

There is a **Universal Law of Problems: All problems grow and accrue interest over a period of time.**

When is the best time to fix a problem? Before it even happens. Changing your oil, while not fun or glamorous, is way easier than replacing an engine.

If you or your customer is even a little bit of a procrastinator, or feeling too busy to look at the onboarding process, you might both be tempted to postpone. Again, getting the whole team involved to lock you into this process will help keep you and your customers on track with the best shot of long-term success, even with some short-term discomfort.

List out the stages of your onboarding process for them. Tell them their minimum requirements for participation in order to get the outcomes they want, and be serious about it. When my Oral Surgeon, Dr. Bahat, told me to "Ice, ice, ice!" after every surgery, I took him very seriously, and quickly invested the time and energy to be rotating ice packs 10 minutes on and off throughout of my waking hours. Every time I saw him for a follow-up, he said: "Looks great. Keep icing." I followed his instructions to a T. You have to be an active participant in your own salvation. That includes your customers.

UNIVERSAL LAW OF PROBLEMS

All problems grow and become more difficult to deal with over a period of time. The best time to deal with a problem is...

4. Talk Internally first about the new customer, or new project, before talking to the customer in depth.

At almost every company I have worked with, there is a regular discussion in the ops department about how haphazard the sales team is. Often, at those same companies, the sales team is complaining because the ops department can't keep up with the workload, and they're operationally disorganized, or inefficient, or shorthanded… or blah, blah, blah.

I don't know or care who is right. They're probably *both* right, to a degree. What I *do* care about is everyone executing on an agreed-upon process to help the ops team and the sales team look like heroes in the eyes of the customer.

As we are about to win, or immediately after we win, I want the lead salesperson to run an internal meeting and follow this agenda in thirty minutes or less.

- Share the Name, key contacts, and promises made to the customer.
- Review the reasons why they hired us.
- Point out your fears about what could go wrong.
- Get your internal team's honest assessment of where we will likely have problems
- Ask them "What am I not seeing?" & "What is the customer not seeing?"
- Develop a list of potential change orders, scope expansion, and expedite fees.

- Discuss the long-term potential for the account and highly likely services that we could offer them in the future
- Draw out the customer org chart as you know it today, and align it to your special teams players.
- Assign them the task of adding to the org chart in a particular area.
- Agree on the schedule for deployment
- Schedule your next 3 meetings with the client and the onboarding team
- Share potential referral possibilities both internally at the new customer, and externally.
- Set a 3rd year revenue goal with the team.
- Thank your team for their efforts.
- Clarify under what circumstances you need to be called back in.
- Get out of their way.

5. Establish the cadence to your kickoff process and get it on the calendar!

Is this three one-hour meetings on Zoom over the next 3-6 weeks, is it one day on-site a week for the first 90 days, is it a 90 minute kick-off with their whole team and your whole team?

Normally, the last one is my preference. 90-minute initial kick off with their whole team and ours. It might not be everybody there the whole time, but it gives you a chance to brag about your team. Point out what they all bring to the table, and why the customer needs to do exactly what they tell them to do in order to be successful.

Self-promotion is basically worthless. Nobody believes you, they discount what you say, and it probably hurts you more than it helps you.

However, you can talk about other people's capabilities with conviction and lean into why they are in their role and how much your **Special Teams** players will be able to help them if the customer just cooperates. Your customers are much more likely to follow your direction now that they are committed, and you have a honeymoon period where you and your customers are both stary-eyed hoping this goes really well. If you don't use this time for maximum effect, the moment may pass, and once things start to not go well, everything you tell the customer will get challenged.

I want to add in here that tonality is key. Remember before when I said you can say anything to anybody if you just say it right? This is a place where that definitely matters. I always like you to have a relaxed confidence. Humble and confident is the perfect mix. Your facial expressions, your body language all matter here. Not too dictatorial, however appropriately authoritative.

If you want to hear how this sounds, head to *chrisjenningsgroup.com* for some examples.

6. External Kick off meeting number #1

You are basically going to take your notes from everything you covered with your internal team and use that as an outline to ensure success. Remind them that it's your job to make this the best experience they have ever had. It's their job to follow your instructions, and if they do, you can virtually guarantee a great outcome.

7. Manage Expectations

Before you get too high and mighty about how you are all going to swoop in and save the day...please, please, please manage expectations!

Like I have mentioned a few times now. Happiness is achieved any time results and outcomes outperform expectations. Anytime something bad didn't happen is a win. Describing all the bad things that could happen, while perhaps a bit scary to you both, sets you both up for lots of wins.

- Let's go back to Mark and his new banker. What could go wrong?

- The bank or their printer could be delayed in mailing out Mark's new checks.

- His payroll company might not be notified of the switch, and he bounces all his first payroll checks.

- He doesn't set up his 3rd party authentication and his accounts get hacked in the first 90 days of switching over.

- He opted not to take the complimentary line of credit he was offered, and his credit score goes down because he has used up the majority of his available credit.

- He has vendors that were not advised of the switch and have not deposited his checks and by the time they deposit the checks he has too small a balance to cover it, the old bank is bummed because he left and doesn't call him, he bounces the check to the vendor, the vendor cuts him off, and he is now late on his shipments to his customer.

Now, most of those things probably *won't* go wrong, but like I said, everything that doesn't go wrong is a win for you if you call it out early. Everything that happens that you *did* call out will have less sting and less negative impact to your relationship, but everything that goes wrong that you *didn't* call out will be your fault, and definitely will negatively impact your relationship. Everything you call out early makes you look like more of the experienced pro that you are, versus a rookie that didn't even know any better than to mention these things in advance.

All of the things on that list happen all the time in banking changeovers, which is partially why customers stick with banks they don't like, because it's such a hassle to switch. Payroll companies, software, accounting, insurance, and on and on and on. So if you make it easier, and the referrals you get mention what an amazing job you did with your onboarding, you are bound to win more business and do more with the customers you already got.

CHRIS
JENNINGS
GROUP

Sample List of Common Customer Problems

Company Name _____   Date _____

- Late on first order
- Miscommunicate pricing
- Additional Charges
- Wrong measurements/take offs
- Overtime charges incurred
- Scope incomplete
- New information added after the start of the project
- New team members introduced/Client/Service Provider
- Supply chain shortages
- Broken/Damaged product
- Misused product
- Team members missed onboarding
- _____
- _____
- _____
- _____
- _____

---

8. Ask what a win looks like for them

After all this unearthing unexpected problems, I think it will help your customer and you as well to reset both your eyes on the target. You probably could and should be able to articulate this for them at this point, but it's a bigger deal if it comes from their mouths, not yours. Also, they may add some additional outcomes that hadn't been emphasized before and maybe you expand the project before

SUCCESSFUL ONBOARDING OF NEW PROJECTS AND CUSTOMERS

it starts? In either case, you both get to refocus on the shortest and best pathway to their new desired outcomes and future state. At this point, they're as excited and confident in you as they will perhaps ever be. You haven't made any mistakes yet. Your team hasn't let them down yet, and you at this moment are a perfect supplier/partner to them.

So, before the magic moment fades, make sure to take the following crucial final steps!

9. Paint the picture of what the future could look like

They hired you to do X, you would love to do Y & Z for them, and perhaps start over with the alphabet and run it all the way back to more X?

I mentioned previously that if most companies did everything they could for every customer they had, they would at least double in size without ever getting another new customer. The more they worked together, the easier it would get to receive orders and deliver on the goods and services promised. The customers you worked with wouldn't have to waste any time getting multiple quotes, and they could just focus their energies on servicing their clients. It would streamline their lives, our lives, and their customers' lives, and so on. Think win-win-win! My favorite.

Now, perhaps your head is trying to talk you out of this, and you're thinking, *The timing isn't right. It's too soon to start asking for more stuff,* *we just invoiced them for $100k of other stuff; how greedy are we going to come across?* You wouldn't be the only one with those thoughts.

I am not saying break out a PO for the next $100k order—but I *am* saying to at least put it on the radar that this is something they might want to consider. If you are a payroll company and they just switched to your payroll service, but not the retirement plan, then I would at least mention that is something you guys are good at doing.

Don't say this...
"I really need to win your Retirement Plan Business." or "What's it going to take for me to win your Retirement Planning, too?" or "It's probably costing you a lot of money to not meet with our retirement people."

All of that is pretty obnoxious, no matter how silky-smooth you deliver it. Hey, if you have a way of delivering things, and you say something like I just said not to say and it works the vast majority of the time, then maybe it fits you and your personality. But for the vast majority of us...

Say this instead...
"Hey Jess, I know we have a bunch to get through with your payroll transfer, and we're on it. At some point

down the road, if you're open to it, we should have a more thoughtful conversation about your retirement planning and administration—if you're open to it?"

Or: "I don't know what your relationship is like with your retirement planning company you use, and if it is the greatest group you have ever worked with, I certainly don't want to get in the way of that. But on the off chance that our team has some ideas about how to make everything easier for you and your people when it comes to Retirement planning and advice, I thought it might at least be worth an exploratory call. Perhaps sometime next quarter, once we're through this. Does that make sense to you, or am I off base here?"

Either of those options are way more low-key, appropriate, and worthy of multiple attempts.

If you have done all that, there is only one thing left to do.

10. Referrals and getting doors opened for you that would stay otherwise closed, or unknown.

Remember Mark and the banker? Here is what their onboarding messaging sounded like.

Say something like this...

"Mark, I do appreciate the vote of confidence in working with us, I know there are a bunch of banks out there, and it matters to me personally that you went with us. I have to tell you that if you and I are completely in sync, the next 90 days will go a lot smoother, and with minimal headaches for you and my team.

So, here's what I suggest. Let's get a weekly call lined up each week for the next 3 months, I am inviting 4 of my key team members to these to make sure that nothing is missed on our end, and I would like you to bring your bookkeeper, CFO, payroll administrator, and benefits administrator. Did I miss anybody?

I'm envisioning us working together for a very long time, and the main things that go wrong on a switch are the following: we didn't get every employee's bank information, the CPA isn't alerted to the change and the tax deposits aren't made, or there is a third party verification required for the first deposit, and it ends up getting in late.

My job is to adequately train your team so none of that happens. Your job is to get your entire team there every week on every one of those calls. If they miss them, we will record them, but they have to review the recording. Are you with me?

If we get 2 months into this, and your team is not participating, and that leads to a problem that was avoidable, neither one of us is going to be happy.

Just so you know, I'm going to be bending over backwards to avoid all these problems, and make you look like a genius for switching banks. My hope is that over time, you are sharing how well we turned out for you with every CEO/business owner you know. Are you good with that? Hey if you already have done so, let me know so I can look out for them.

If so, let's get started.

By the way, I know you wanted to start with your business assets only, I think at some point we should have a more thoughtful conversation about why we might want to look at your personal assets. Not today, but maybe at our first Quarterly Business Review, does that sound in any way appealing?"

I've already given you some ideas here. My goal is to get you comfortable enough to bring this up at least 80% of the time. You can keep tweaking the language until it suits you in a really positive way.

I am going to devote an entire section to getting referrals, making that conversation easier for you, easier for you clients, and easier for those new customers you don't even know exist. Before I go there on referrals, I would like to chip away and continue to sculpt your story so that it's exactly the right one to tell your customers.

## FIVE

WHAT'S YOUR STORY?

One of the companies I'm currently working with is a Kitchen and Bath Remodeler. They employ a team of senior designers, people at the top of their craft. At a sales meeting a couple of weeks ago, one of their designers, Roxanne, pulled me aside.

"I don't know if I'm cut out for Special Teams," she said, her voice full of tension. "I'm not a salesperson. I'm a designer. I don't know what to say to customers that is going to help them hire us."

I hear this from Special Teams members all the time, and it's completely understandable. Relatable, even; who on Earth wants to be known as or thought of as a salesperson? A designer sounds so much more refined, professional, and credible in their environment.

Here's the problem. If you're telling yourself the story, "This isn't who I am. This isn't what I do," then you're bound to prove yourself right. It's a self-fulfilling prophecy. You'll probably find a lot less business, and make a lot less money, and get to help a lot fewer customers, than if you got your mind to a healthier place that serves you better for the situation you're in.

Before we get into the "scary" content in this book—directly asking for referrals—I felt it important to help you as the reader consider your own stories that you carry around. So often when I am coaching a team of professionals, they have a long list of reasons why not. Reasons why they can't ask for referrals, that it's not their job to expand the account, and before I give you any more specific strategies around how to grow and maintain great relationships with clients, I wanted to give you some tools to prepare your mind, to accept an even better future than your past. Rewiring our thinking to help us accomplish our goals is an important step in improving the quality of our working lives, and often our personal lives as well.

Everybody tells themselves stories. The question is: are you rooting for yourself to succeed, being your own biggest fan, encouraging yourself to move forward, learn, grow, and evolve?

Or: are you mired down in self-doubt, expecting the worst, overcome by fear, and second-guessing everything you do? Are you spending your days looking for evidence to prove yourself right, rendering yourself less effective?

I hope it's the first one. However, even the most evolved individuals still carry some self-doubt. Some self-limiting programming that you inherited from your family, your friends, the news broadcast, a social media post, a former boss, partner, spouse. Our tendency as self-doubting humans is to cut off our nose to spite our face, and I see it all the time in the companies I work with.

I have another question for you: why are you listening to these stories?

Consider the negative consequence of carrying around all that baggage. What could you be capable of, if you weren't burdened by all that heavy crud of limitation, despair, and victimhood that weighs you down and makes functioning in life more difficult?

This chapter is dedicated to cleaning up your mind and creating space for the goals, thought process, and positive self-encouragement that will be necessary to make forward progress.

I told Roxanne that day: "I do think you can be a great salesperson. I do believe that lots of people will pay you for your advice and hire you to oversee their remodel project. The problem is, it doesn't matter what I think. It is critical what *you* think." Her story was going to have to evolve to reach her full true potential.

Another client of mine, Mark, started as a driver for a large distribution firm. He could have easily settled into that role and spent his entire career there. Totally cool, if that is what he loves to do—but he wanted more. He believed he could do more. He was willing to grow and push himself to acquire new skills.

He got promoted to sales, where he performed well. He saw that he had even more in him; he became a sales manager. Wanted more. He became the VP of sales. Envisioned himself going even further. He eventually became the president of the company.

Now, he didn't just think his way into those roles. He *worked* his way into those roles. However, I submit that none of that success would have likely come to pass had he not *believed* it could. The stories he developed internally, backed up by the work that he did to grow, is what led to his incredible advancement.

A TEN STEP PROCESS FOR WRITING YOUR BEST STORY

1. Set a Goal

What are your top three goals? These could be both personal and business.

Ask yourself: what do you want? We live in a world of unlimited opportunity. So imagine a future different from your present. What do you want to see in that future?

Business examples could include:

- Double your sales in the next 3 years
- Ask every client for a referral each visit
- Leading your department
- Completing a course in a new skill
- Meeting one new person a month at every client you serve
- Ride along/shadow a member of a different department for a day

Personal goals might look like:

- Go on the family vacation you've been dreaming about
- Learn a new language.
- Hit the gym 4 times per week
- Take an art class, or Pilates class, or fire walking (whatever floats your boat!)
- Donate a half day a week to the local Rescue Mission
- Tackle one cleaning/home improvement project per month

Once you've defined your goals, take stock of what's in the way.

THE CLIENT RETENTION MATRIX

2. Write Out Your 3 Biggest Obstacles

Meeting goals isn't easy; if it was, we wouldn't have them. There will always be obstacles, complex situations with natural barriers. Identify what they are in the most objective and neutral tone you can.

Maybe you're a project manager/floor lead for a fastener company. The sales team brings in orders with consistently tight deadlines that make it difficult or impossible to meet customer demands, but you never get invited to the onboarding meeting for the project, and all you feel is pressure from sales, under what feels like unrealistic objectives. That wouldn't surprise me, and it's a huge obstacle.

Maybe you set a personal goal to run a 10k this summer, but you keep getting out of work late and don't have time to train. That's a big obstacle.

Once you've identified your top 3 obstacles, you need to create a pathway forward, and a clear way out of the old thinking.

3. Create Your Goal Board

You've seen these before. Goal boards. Vision boards. A pictorial representation of what the future holds for you. Visualize yourself getting that degree you are working towards, in the office you want, living in a new home that you bought on the vacation where you want, earning the kind of living you want.

Get the photos, build it on cut out boards, an online whiteboard, or however you want. Paint the picture of your new future. A year out, 5 years out, 10 years out. There is so much life to be experienced. Please create the one you are wanting with the people you want to be with.

4. Build the Plan

One of the keys to accomplishing goals is having a very simple plan that will inch you closer to your goals. It won't always be forward progress. We won't always take the action we need. But coming back to the basics, and having a plan, will get you there in the long run.

For example, my plan for writing this book, as well as my other two books, was to write every time I was on an airplane. As I'm writing this, I'm currently sitting on a flight, and I spent the first couple hours getting in a nap after an early takeoff. When I woke up, I opened back up my laptop and I'm committed to finishing this section by the time we land.

Let's say you're the project manager who wants face time with clients before the project starts. Here's your plan:

- Get copied on all proposals with a 90% chance of closing and read the SOW (Scope of Work)
- Ask the Salesperson, and/or Sales Manager for the lifetime potential business from this client
- List out your Top 5 criteria for a successful fulfilment of all the promises made.

- Offer a contingency plan for when things don't go as planned.

You want to run a 10K in April to support a fundraiser, but you haven't gone running since high school. That's a hell of an uphill battle, but you've got a plan.

- Buy some new comfortable running shoes.
- Identify 3 days a week and a time slot that will become your dedicated training time.
- Start with walking for 30 minutes at a doable pace. Slowly each week increase the time, and the pace.
- Pick out a great audiobook to listen to while you train—better yet, a book series.
- Ask somebody to join you/meet you at the dedicated time and place. Accountability partners supercharge any journey to a goal.

5. Share Your Goals with Someone Else

Secret goals that you never share, and never get down on paper, are really just ideas floating around your head. They get lost in your head along with the myriad of ideas, and old habits, and get buried in your mind, like a pile of stuff in a junk drawer that you occasionally look through, but can't find what you want.

Bring your goals out into the light. Share them with at least 5 people in your life. These should be people you live with, work with, and socialize with regularly. Ask for their help to revisit these goals on some regular frequency: monthly, weekly, or even daily.

6. Learn and Acquire the Skills

If there is knowledge you need to be good at your job, acquire it. See if your company has a reimbursement program for learning new skills that will help you at work. Sign up for some classes; keep reading, this book and others. Find a podcast that lets you learn on your drive to work.

Do you have terrible running form? YouTube drills, get a coach, join a running club, and/or see a physical therapist.

The knowledge is out there. No excuses. You're building a new version of yourself that needs to be supported.

7. Write Out Your New Story

Get your new story on paper. Write out the positive version you're growing into, the person accomplishing all your goals. Start with some brainstorming of the goals and obstacles, then rewrite the script as if you either just had accomplished the goals, or you're making progress towards the goals.

Professionally, it might look like this:

- I am enjoying getting to know our customers.
- I am learning so much about our customers and what they want.

- I am becoming more comfortable asking the customers to help us help them.
- Our new project onboarding meetings are becoming very effective for the customers and my team.
- I am enjoying great success as a result of sticking to my plans and my goals.

Personally, it could look like this:

- I am committed to running a 10k every year.
- My body is starting to transform in a positive healthy way.
- I feel stronger every week as a result of sticking to my plan.
- I am growing more confident at work.
- I am enjoying learning 4 new skills per year that help me and my family.
- I am entitled to live a happy, successful, and grateful existence while finding time to fit in all the priorities in my life.
- Each day I grow more content with the accomplishments and progress I am making.

Read these back to yourself and record them with some cool music in the background. Listen to the recording weekly, or daily as needed. Believe in the possibility that your future is better than your past.

Post these affirmations in multiple places that you see each day. Your mirror, your car, your phone, or even your coffee pot.

8. Tell on Yourself When You're Not Sticking to the Process

One of my favorite things to do in life is to tell on myself. I do stupid things from time to time, things that I wish I hadn't. Or I'll fail to do certain things that I meant to do. I don't think that's unusual, and I definitely don't beat myself up over these missteps, other than for perhaps a few seconds. I just try to quickly acknowledge that it happened. I regularly tell others about mistakes I have made, try to get a laugh out of it, a lesson out of it, and know that in my life I get lots of second chances.

Important note: Tell on yourself, but don't beat yourself up.

It's entirely possible that this might be the key to forward progress. Keeping your lack of progress a dark secret that gets buried in the junk drawer, hiding from others our shortcomings, doesn't really give us an opportunity to improve.

Do yourself and others a favor. Be transparent and honest about what you get done and what you don't. Don't give up on goals because of a busy week, or a week that you were sick, or a week that you just didn't have the stamina to do something.

Just try to regroup, refocus, reread the plans, rescan the goal board, and get back on it. It's pretty simple. Easier said than done, but quite simple.

9. Find A Guide Or A Mastermind Group
That Supports Your New Story

All the people you've been hanging around in your life to date have helped shape the person you are today. If you're not the person you want to be today, then maybe you need a guide, a mentor. In fact, you probably need a bunch of them. The cool thing is that you get to pick the crowd. Find a community of people that you respect and aspire to be like.

They may already exist at your work. They could be your college alumni group, or even your neighbors. Start sharing the areas of your life you want to grow in and ask people how they have grown in their own lives. Wisdom is all around, and as the saying goes, "When the student is ready, the teacher will appear."

Did somebody recommend this book to you? Maybe you could ask for their help. Maybe you could seek out a professional coaching organization like ours at *chrisjenningsgroup.com* to sit in on a free program. Maybe you join Toastmasters, Vistage, BNI, or any of the organizations dedicated to personal and professional development. Find an advisory board to hold you accountable and help shape the new you.

10. Commit to The Process

Last but not least, you must commit to the process. Fall in love with the process. Become a master of the process.

Don't get overly concerned with the pace, or size of the outcomes. Get dedicated to your process, and your process will dedicate itself to you.

This is a great life we are given. Embrace the change, the learning, and the struggle until the life you have always dreamed of becomes the life you are living.

10 Laws for Personal Growth

1. **Remain teachable.** Fight the urge to resist learning. It's what you learn after you know it all that counts.
2. **Get comfortable, feeling uncomfortable.** It's okay, it won't kill you. It means you are getting stronger. Progress, not perfection.
3. **Write and rewrite**. Your personal goals and visions you want to create. Reaffirm everything you deserve, even if you don't yet really believe that you do.
4. **Borrow from others that appear stronger.** Act as if you are them. Try on their confidence for size until it is really who you are.
5. **Find a source of strength outside of yourself.** Be it religion, nature, the gym, the piano; create a never-ending well to draw from.
6. **Use the old self-limiting stories** that lie within you as a reminder of what was, and be strong and faithful as you set your new course and rewrite your beliefs.
7. **Be grateful for every lesson that you receive.** Disappointment is always followed by a return to greatness. Take the lesson with grace and humility. Appreciate how far you have come and look with eagerness to who you are becoming.
8. **When your head tells you** not to show up, not to try, or not to commit or that you're already doing that, reframe and ask yourself, how can I do this even better? What simple adjustments could elevate my game to even higher highs?
9. **Stay humble.** There are many teachers all around; your coach, trainer, fellow student, boss, employee, prospect, child, parent, and random encounters are all brought to you to teach you something. Your job is to discover the lesson.
10. **Embrace sacrifice.** Invest in yourself. Give yourself the time - you are worth the investment. Even if it is hard to do, it all will bring you so much more. Open your mind to your future self. Let your dreams materialize; they always will, if you work for them.

chrisjenningsgroup.com

SIX

ALL ABOUT REFERRALS

My favorite way to do business is to work with somebody I already know, or get a referral that somebody else I know already has trust and respect for.

Maybe you read my first book on sales and sales leadership and have been working really hard to get better conversion rates on leads that you get or cold calls that you make. Yes, they all work, and well done on your efforts. However, no group of opportunity will ever convert at a higher rate, with a shorter sales cycle, with a lower cost of sales,

THE CLIENT RETENTION MATRIX

than getting referrals and introductions from clients that have already worked with you and can give personal testimony to the effectiveness with which you delivered your product or services.

Plus, it's how people *want* to buy. They want to know who the best providers are and get their problems solved quickly, after a short an easy connection is facilitated by a trusted referral source. This is, once again, a win-win-win.

If you want to count yourself among the most successful people out there, you're going to become a *connector*, and start to receive lots of connections as a result.

My friend and client Clay has long been one of the more consistently successful sales professionals I've worked with in his industry. He has about the perfect combination of smarts, confidence, and humility. While Clay has great skills in both sales and sales leadership, I know a lot of his success has come from his reputation and the number of connections he has developed along the way. He's super disciplined about making sure he asks for referrals and that his teams do the same. It's a winning formula.

What I've noticed is that there is a tipping point in one's career based on the number of good connections you have. I define a good connection as a current or former customer, or colleague that if you called them and left them a voicemail, they would definitely call you back. Now, when I first met Clay, he probably already had about 100 such connections. He regularly got easy business by growing with his colleagues, and as they took on larger roles and were in better positions to make buying decisions his pathway to success got easier and easier. Today I would guess that Clay has over 500 connections like that. (By the way, ideally, if you're tracking this in LinkedIn, here's your qualifier for deciding whether someone should be a connection in LinkedIn or not: would they call you back if you left them a voicemail?)

Depending on your industry, the tipping point for how many connections you need in order to have an unlimited supply of business coming in is between 250 and 500. Generally speaking, at that level, you're getting at least a call or email per week saying, "Hey, I was referred to you by_____, and I would like to talk to you about using your services." Once you get to that level, it is really hard not to write tons of business.

So, the question is this: how many of those types of connections do you really have today, and is it going to take you forty more years to get to where you need to be, or can you do it in four years?

Ask yourself: do you have a referral process that you follow at least 80% of the time? If you don't, time to get busy.

If you're already breaking out into a sweat because this topic makes you so nervous, just go back to the last section, get your story straight, and then come back here to dial this in. If you're eagerly awaiting the plan for how best to do this, keep reading.

There are three basic categories of referrals I'm going to talk you through, and then we'll do some cleanup with a few others that might apply to you as well.

1. Referrals from new and existing clients
2. Referrals from Strategic Partners and other Centers of Influence
3. Referrals from personal contacts, friends, family and others

Unfortunately, as I wrote earlier, most of us never proactively ask for referrals. My goal here is to start to make this process so easy for you that you not only don't break a sweat when asking, but because you're so comfortable with the ask, your audience wants to oblige your request with a referral to someone who could really use your help.

REFERRALS FROM NEW AND EXISTING CLIENTS

These should be asked for during the onboarding process for every new client, and every new project for an existing client.

I'm convinced this is your best time to start the process. I know some of you might still be freaking out at the idea; you fear that this early in the relationship, you haven't earned the right, and you think you'll come off as inappropriate and presumptuous and send your clients running off screaming into the night.

Think about it, though: you took the client/project on because you saw yourself as a great solution to their issues. You're confident you can help them. Bringing up the referral at the very start only magnifies your confidence in the outcomes your client will be experiencing.

Don't say this...

"I could really use some new people to call on and anybody you know that could benefit from our services I would treat them very well and even throw you a rebate back on the services you just bought from us." No! Sounds very salesy to me, and bluntly offering to buy referrals with discounts feels inappropriate.

Say this instead...

"I so appreciate the vote of confidence in hiring us. I think you will see myself, and our entire organization, working really hard to get the outcomes we both want here—which we are doing for a couple of reasons: one, there are a lot of things that we could be doing together, and two, we're hoping that eventually you will want to work with us, and perhaps only us.

Additionally, I'm counting on you to be so impressed with how we work that you want to connect us to people that you naturally run into that I would probably never meet without your help. I just wanted to know if you were open to that." Or "I just wanted to know if that sounds okay to you?"

The vast majority of people are going to say "Sure, happy to do that."

Here's an important note: too many of us will check the box, and say to ourselves, "Well, I asked, but didn't get anything." But wait—you're not done! Effective referral gathering requires a conversation with 2-5 different requests that follow seamlessly in the same conversation.

Ask multiple times in the same conversation, and over multiple conversations. This is not a one and done scenario. Just like most college ball players who leave college too soon and aren't fully ready for the NBA, but leave college thinking they are ready when they are not, a single solitary request, in and of itself, is unlikely to warrant the results you want.

So, after they say, "Sure, I would be happy to help," the follow-up dialogue sounds like this...

"Great, I really appreciate that. Out of curiosity, where do you think those people would come from?"

This, to me, is a much better question than "Who do you know?", which is the more popular often-asked question. Some of you can get that to work, but a lot of us end up stalling out with the client responding, "I can't think of anybody, but I will for sure let you know." Which almost never happens.

Make referrals easier for you to ask for, and for them to take action on. I don't think people are reluctant to refer you, I think they stumble on figuring out how to do it. Make it your job to make it easier for them. One of the ways to do that is to ask **where the referral** would come from; it gets them thinking along the path of who they know who might benefit from your services. Additionally, to make it easier, you may need to suggest where these people would likely come from.

Say something like this...
"Would these be people you work with in another department, people you used to work with at another company, people you know from a business group you're in like a Vistage group, or industry function that you go to regularly? Where do you think they would come from?"

Start to get more details about the places they spend time in, and the likely referral sources that they'll encounter. As they're describing the various affiliations of professional and personal groups, take lots of notes. You probably won't get everything you could from them in one conversation, and you'll need to revisit this topic again, and again, and again.

Be prepared to list all the groups, communities, business and personal that your referring party might likely be associated with. Like I said, this might be a multi-step ask, and having notes of all the places they spend their time will make it easier for them to help you.

Also try this question: "Anybody coming to mind in particular, **first names only?**"

First names only softens the request considerably. It takes away your customers' fear that you will be showing up at their friend's doorstep the next morning with your hand out looking for business.

It allows them to talk openly without getting hung up in what you might do next.

If they start to mention actual people they know that you could help, stay calm, let the game come to you, and don't rush your shot.

> **Don't say this...**
> "Great, I would really like to get a hold of them and demonstrate our capabilities ASAP, as I think we're about to have a price increase." Please, don't threaten your clients into a referral.

Say this instead...

"So you mention Carley, Becca, and Joel. What made you think of them?"

Let them come up with some good reasons why you might be able to help them, get some details. Take your time. Try not to appear overly eager, greedy, or any other off-putting weirdness that will shut down the natural flow of the dialogue. Get them to convince you that they might need the help.

Then simply state, "I'm happy to help them if I can. What do you think is the best way for us to connect? Would you want to arrange a lunch, give them a call first, or are you thinking of connecting us via a simple email?"

Connect us, not *refer* us. This is important. I mentioned earlier that the word I never like to use when asking for a referral is "referral".

Keep it simple and ask for them to connect you. That is what human beings want—to be connected to other human beings. It satisfies some basic needs of community and promotes safety in the connection. Whereas a referral has fear-baggage attached to it.

If you really hate asking, just tell them that. It's important to be your most authentic self. So if asking makes you a bit squeamish, tell them the truth.

I've got a client named Micah, a super talented tax and investment expert. He's not sales oriented at all, but luckily for his business, he doesn't need to be. He's so talented and gives such tremendously insightful financial info to his clients that they all love him. They look for opportunities to refer him. He, like a lot of people, doesn't like asking for things for himself.

Don't say this...

"I know how obnoxious it is every time you get asked for something. It bugs me a lot, too, but I could really use some referrals."

Say this instead...

"Hey Chris, I've really appreciated getting to work with you, and there has been something I've been meaning to bring up, but I haven't figured out a good way to ask. Frankly, I feel sort of awkward even asking." At this point They're going to be dying to know what it is. "I know we've been working together for a while now, and I've never even mentioned how much it would mean to me if you connected me to other people you know who could use the kind of help I offer. I just wanted to know if you would be cool with that?"

The vast majority of the people are going to say, "Yes, absolutely, how can I help?" It's really pretty straight forward, if you just simply tell people the truth. The truth resonates with all of us, immediately, and it inspires people to act.

Say something like this...
"I've always been really good with numbers, investment strategies, and tax law. The thing I've never been really good at or felt at all comfortable doing was asking people like you to connect me with others that need this kind of help. In fact, I'm starting to regret that I even brought this up."

Often, the more vulnerable the better. It just has to be authentic.

Do not use this as a strategy to manipulate people. If you're super confident asking, then use any of the other strategies—don't fake vulnerability.

Here are some more strategies. Try to find 2–3 in this chapter that work for you, and make them your go-tos.

"Who have you told about us?"
Again, if this fits, run with it. Odds are that your clients have talked to their friends about their success with you and or your firm, and

when they offered to give them your contact info, the referral said, "No, that's ok. I can find them online."

Now, maybe they can, but the point is, if they can't find you, or get distracted and lose interest due to life taking over, they may forget down the road about you. Then when they remember, they might search some random company and find whoever they thought was you—which might be your biggest competitor, who is probably not nearly as good as you are.

Say something like this...
"So Bill, who have you told about us?" If the answer is *nobody*, well—uh oh! That's a problem. By the way, I would say exactly that to your client. They're going ask why it's a problem, and you can respond with, "It's making me nervous that you aren't telling people about us. Are we letting you down somehow?"

"I'm concerned I've done something wrong."
It's along the same theme as the last one; you're just getting there faster. Just another alternate for you to try. Please remember to pick the ones that are more authentically you. If not, it'll come out wrong, and you'll create a problem where there wasn't one.

I've had people come tell me about their success with referrals, and sometimes, I've felt like they were trying too hard. Like I said, let the game come to you.

Don't say this...

"I'm really starting to wonder if you truly value this relationship. By this time, I've normally gotten bunches of referrals. Where have I gone wrong?" Again, too strong. Too much salt ruins the taste. Season appropriately without over seasoning.

Say this instead...

"Hey Wanda. Can I ask you something? I've been starting to wonder if you feel like we're doing a good enough job for you?" They're likely to respond with some version of, *I love working with you, why would you think that?* "Normally by now, somewhere along the way, if I'm doing at least a good job, there is typically somebody else that you have talked to about us that comes looking for help. Since that hadn't happened yet, I was starting wonder how you felt I was doing?"

Again, make this your words, not necessarily mine, but work this theme into the mix.

You can also say this: "Maybe I haven't done a good job of bringing this up, which is totally on me."

Keep it real, see where it goes, no need to force anything here. A similar variation to this is...

"I've been meaning to ask you..."
This is a close cousin to the prior idea. It's especially appropriate for busy customers that you see or talk to often, who are often rushing from one thing to the next.

> **Say something like this...**
> "I've been meaning to ask you something and feeling a little embarrassed that I never brought this up." Again, they're going to want to know. "I generally am introduced to just about everybody that I work with, and I'm not sure that I've even mentioned how important that is to me. Getting connected to the people that you're naturally running into who typically need the kind of help I offer that I would never meet without your help is super important to me, and I wondered if you were open to talking about this a little?"

You can layer multiple tactics together. As long as it represents how you feel, and you keep it very authentic, it'll work.

If you've read up to this point and can feel yourself pushed out of your comfort zone, *good*. I spent the whole prior section prepping you to get pushed, and I promise to address some of the questions that I guess are right about now rattling around your head.

"I could really use your help."

People like to help other people. It makes us feel good about ourselves to do something nice for another person. Especially if that person has been particularly helpful to us. It evens the score in some ways and satisfies our psychological need to be in balance.

Now, not every strategy is going to work with every customer. Don't freak out if you aren't seeing immediate success. There's a good chance your delivery is off, or your internal conviction regarding the strategy isn't strong enough yet. I absolutely promise that if you stick to the process, and fall in love with the process, the process will love you back.

Don't say this...

"Hey Alice, I'm really struggling here, and I definitely need some more clients. Who do you have I can start calling on?" Look, if by some miracle, you're saying that, and it's working—bless you. It's probably because of your tonality and conviction towards the process. It's not going to work for most people, and I don't recommend it.

Say this instead...
"Alice, can I ask you something? I could really use
some help figuring out better ways to meet new
people that I could help. I love what I do, and I'm
pretty dependent on getting help from clients like
you that know my work best. I just wondered if you
would be open to having that discussion?" Keep it
simple.

Here's a potential add-on to this strategy: "As much as I don't like
asking you to connect me to other people I can help, if I don't do it,
I end up needing to call strangers for a living, and I absolutely hate
that even more. Have you ever had to do that?"

I promise you, you will get a lot of empathy here, and once again,
relatability. Your customers might even share stories of their own
former hardest to-dos in their career, and this should lead to a very
productive and fruitful conversation.

As a reminder, combine these freely as they occur to you, and see
what resonates with you and your customers.

"Don't keep us a secret."
The reality is that all of us human beings are busy. We're preoccupied
with thoughts of ourselves and our own lives. Sometimes we need
a little shakeup to get out of that self-centeredness. In this instance,

you're giving your customer a directive; depending on your tonality, it's almost an order.

I'm going to guess that most of you are regularly doing things to help your customers in ways beyond the normal call of duty. Driving across the county, state, or country; expediting something they forgot to account for; not up charging them for the "extras" they asked for on the job.

When your customer says, "I can't thank you enough," instead of just replying, "My pleasure" or "Happy to help":

Say something like this...

"I'm really glad we were able to get this done for you. If you meant what you said, perhaps I could ask you for something?" They will likely say *absolutely, anything you need*. You can then respond with:

"What would really mean the most to me is if you shared this story with other people that you already know that would appreciate this kind of help. I'm not sure I ever mentioned how big a deal it is for me when I get introduced to new people from my clients like you, and I wondered if you would be open to that?"

By the way, it's important to get every customer-facing individual on your team, especially all your Special Teams Players, very comfortable with this concept. Odds are, you won't be the one there when those favors are being doled out, but you should be capitalizing on the overall team effort to help your customer.

It's really important to take advantage of the multiplier effect. You worked so hard to get that first customer, at an extremely high acquisition cost—you need to multiply the effect.

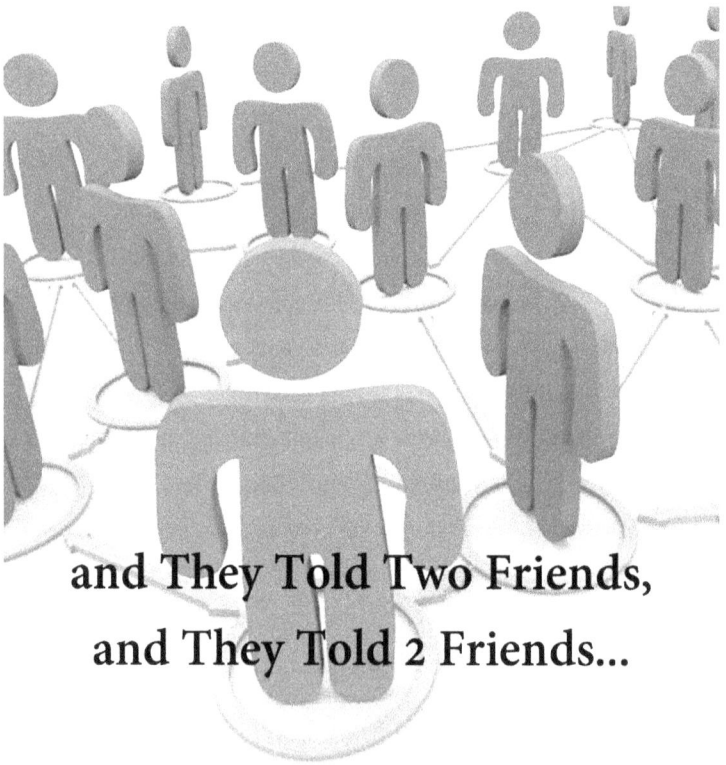

and They Told Two Friends,
and They Told 2 Friends...

Otherwise, you'll likely never accomplish nearly as much as you could. Don't deprive yourself of the success you could enjoy due to fear or awkwardness. Work harder at making the conversation easier to have for both you and your customer.

"Next time we're together."

This is one to try if you're having a hard time having the conversation in the moment due to them being in a hurry. Maybe you just bailed them out of a problem, maybe time is short, and you're not going to have enough time to make a dent in the conversation.

Say something like this...

"Glad we could help, and it means a lot to me that you trust us with helping you. Maybe next time we're together, we could save 5 or 10 minutes to talk a bit about other people you may have thought of that we could help, that I might not ever meet without you connecting us? Would you be open to that?" They're going to say yes. "Great, I'm going to hold you to that. Out of curiosity, where would they come from? Would they be people from other divisions, former colleagues, alumni pals..."

"I get paid in two different ways."

With this one, it's very important to get the tonality just right. To be clear, it's *always* important to get the tonality right, but particularly with this strategy. Keep it light and honest.

Say something like this...

"Hey Jon. Thanks for the trust in working with us. I will be sending you an invoice later today. I wanted to tell you that we do get paid in two different ways. First, I'll appreciate you getting the invoice into accounting for prompt payment. And second, I count on getting introduced to new people that you naturally come in contact with that I would never have met without your help, and I wanted to see if I could count on you."

I know you can have this conversation if it resonates with you. But if it doesn't, don't force it. If you're needing clarity on this or any of the referral suggestions in this chapter, check out the videos and sessions at *chrisjenningsgroup.com*.

Ok, I only have two left for the time being. Both of these may intimidate you at first, but both will likely work 100% of the time if delivered with the right tonality. If you're feeling unsure, just skip ahead to the next section. If you're ready to really step this up a notch or two, then try to work these in to your conversations somehow.

"I'm too old, too tired, and completely consumed by helping you."

I was out for breakfast one day with my friend and client, Larry, just catching up on work, life, and everything in between. He asked me for my thoughts on the best way for him to get referrals, so I shared this with him.

I said, "Larry, you've been around awhile, I'm sure your clients love you, and think the world of you. If I were in your shoes, I would just tell them the truth. I would say: "Guys, I'm too old and too tired to run around town knocking on doors looking for new people to work with. I just can't do it. The only way I get to keep doing this, though, is to make sure that we have new people coming to us so I can stay 100% focused on you, your issues, and your goals. In order for me to do that, I need your help."

Larry was skeptical, but he gave it a try. Lo and behold, his clients jumped into action and loaded up his calendar with prospects.

You see, sometimes, we want to create the illusion of endless success with our clients, and asking for referrals feels like breaking that facade. But it never fails to simply tell the truth. Do it nicely. Tell them how it also impacts them, not just you.

This next one is a winner. Ninety-five percent of you will never try this, even though I'm telling you that it works 100% of the time—and I don't say that very often.

"Get out your cell phone."

One of the reasons we don't get referrals even when we do ask is that customers struggle to recall the names of people they would like to introduce you to. It's not that they don't want to help. It's probably because the request caught them off guard—because you haven't conditioned them to know how important it is.

I remember working with a group of people who sold contact lenses via doctors' offices by getting the doctors to recommend their product. I offered this suggestion in the middle of a two-day kickoff meeting we ran for their team. The idea was received with the typical skepticism, but a few team members said they'd try it.

At our next session, a sales pro named Lindsay said, "Chris, I did what you suggested. I was visiting one of my docs that I see regularly..."

She asked if the doctor was up for trying something new, and he said, "Sure."

"Great," she replied. "Do you have your cell phone handy?" He did. "Open up your contacts, and just start at the A's and scroll. If you come across anybody in there that you think I could help, stop and tell me their first name."

As Lindsey recounted to us, "He was only at the C's when I already had 9 new people to call. I've already seen 3 of them and immediately got 2 new clients."

Nothing is going to work as well as that (that I know of). Like I said before, this will probably work best for clients that you know well and want to help you succeed, which, if you're running your Client Retention Matrix properly, is most of them. Again, the key here is you believing enough in yourself and what you do first, so that you communicate these referral concepts the appropriate way.

"I'm counting on this working out really well for you!"

This works best very early in the engagement process. Tell the client, "We're both in this together. I need you to have some great outcomes with hiring us, so that you go tell all the people you know how great this worked out and that they end up hiring us down the road, when the time is right. Are you okay with that?"

I believe that all relationships need to be win-win-win. I think we should absolutely focus on the successful outcomes that our clients need to experience, and in exchange for that, they graciously introduce us to new people that need the help. It's a win for us, it's a win for the client, and it's a win for the new customer; we get to help solve their issues they were formerly troubled by.

This way, you really can focus your energies appropriately. If you have mutual agreement from the beginning that these are the terms of the relationship, then your clients will appreciate what you bring to the table, you'll get the satisfaction of continuous growth, and you'll very time-efficiently grow your business.

Win
for
Client

Do It

Win
for
Clients'
Customer

Win
for
Service
Provider

Maybe Not Do It

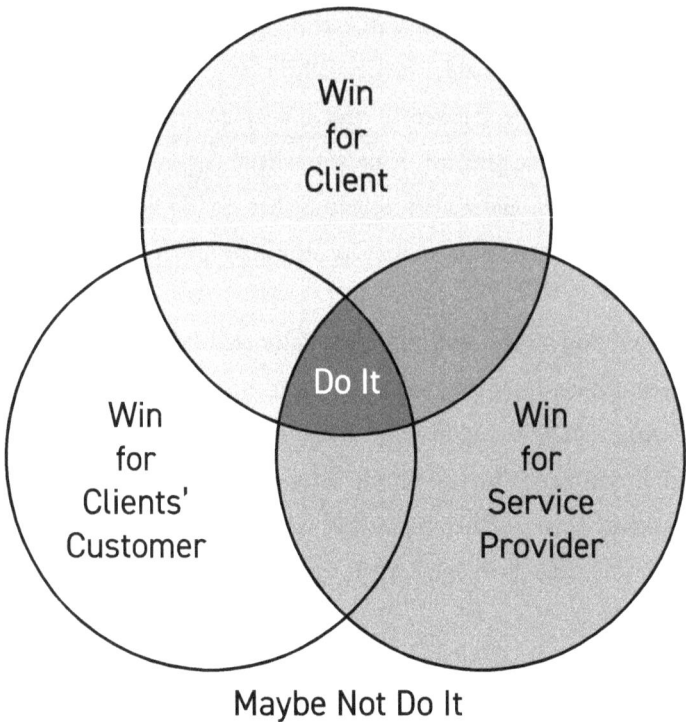

I think for me, this concept really hit home after my divorce. I remember all of a sudden becoming a single dad with shared custody of my three beautiful daughters—which meant I couldn't just work endless hours to grow. I was picking them up from school, making their lunches, and still needing to support my family and maintain all the obligations that I had. It was at that time that I really personally doubled down on this topic and turned up the referral conversation from a friendly request, to more of a serious expectation from anybody that I worked with. Even with less available time to invest, I started to grow again in a significant way.

My recommendation: don't wait for some life changing event to push you down the road in this journey. Just make a start.

The following chart is designed as a summary of all 20 referral strategies. You can also download it at *chrisjenningsgroup.com*.

Referral Guide
How to ask for referrals

1. During the On-Boarding.
2. Multiple times in the same conversation.
3. Referrals easier for you to ask for, and for them to take action.
4. Where would they come from?
5. First names only?
6. If you really hate asking, just tell them that.
7. Who have you told about us?
8. I'm concerned I've done something wrong.
9. I've been meaning to ask you...
10. I could really use your help.
11. If I don't do it, I end up needing to call strangers for a living.
12. Don't keep us a secret.
13. Customers a favor.
14. Next time we are together.
15. I get paid in 2 different ways.
16. I'm too old, too tired, and completely consumed by helping you.
17. Get out your cell phone.
18. I am counting on this working out really well for you!
19. "Connect me"
20.

One last thing before I move on. Please **GoLive!** All of these strategies were designed to occur in a live dialogue.

I'm not saying that you can't follow up with emails, or keep the topic alive in email, but don't be lazy, or afraid, and just randomly start emailing your clients referral requests and expect to have the kinds of results I'm suggesting.

You will know you're doing it right when every day, you get a phone call, text, email, or LinkedIn reach-out that says "Hey, I heard you were really good at such and such, and we need to talk."

REFERRALS FROM STRATEGIC PARTNERS AND OTHER CENTERS OF INFLUENCE

There are several organizations devoted to the concept of networking through other service/solutions providers that call on the same clients that you do. Certainly, it stands to reason that the right strategic partner could be super valuable to you, if they're wired like you are.

However, be prepared to kiss a lot of frogs. Lots of people will tell you that they want to partner, but not all partners are created equal. It's only worthwhile to pursue partners who want to work like you want to work. Know that it may take some time to build the right team around you.

Here is a checklist to help you build a team and navigate this effort.

1. Ask your clients.

Just ask the clients, "Hey, who else do you work with that you rely on as a valued resource?" Get some details from them about who they are, making sure they don't sound like direct competitors. If they sound like a good complementary partner, just ask the client to send you both an introductory email. Make it easy for them and send them the email template.

"Joel, meet Alexys. Alexys and I were talking today about the good work you do for us. She has been providing some great HR & payroll support, and I thought the two of you should connect. I'll let you guys take it from there."

So simple! Now the client is out of it, and you get to start building your dream team of referring partners.

2. Tell your partner what you expect from them.

If you're wanting a dynamic relationship where you get together monthly, share client lists, talk openly about prospects in your pipeline, and proactively bring each other in on deals at least once a month, then set that bar, and be honest.

If you're fine just meeting for lunch every so often, and okay if no business is exchanged, well, that's up to you. At a minimum, set an expectation with each other. If your clients only have opportunities cross their desk once a quarter, be clear about that. If you're just there waiting for the one big opportunity, it may never come, and I want you to be smart with your time.

3. Form a group.

A while back, Lance Riffenburg invited me to speak for a group he helped assemble. It was a bunch of service providers that all offered services closely related to companies that were moving. He had a commercial realtor, a cable provider, a mover, a printer, I think he offered IT services at the time. The point was all of these services would be needed at once if a company was relocating.

You had to bring your prospect list to their meetings, and you had to talk about who you met with and share details of the move. They were being really smart with their time, and the group did a lot of business together.

4. Join a group.

Maybe you aren't up for starting your own, and you're wondering where to go. There are hundreds of such groups meeting in your area right now, and maybe you fit. Provisors, Highrise Networks, BNI, LeTip…the list goes on. Some are more about professional services, some more broad. It will get you started at least.

5. Visit one new group a month.

If networking to build clients through strategic partners is important, keep searching for that newer, better fit organization for you. You may find it in a particular industry association, or other professional development group like Vistage for example.

The goal is to assemble a team of at least a dozen people that in all cases when they encounter somebody with your unique set of requirements, they turn them over to you, and once again, once you're getting a phone call or an email every day from somebody who has been sent to you, your career will be in overdrive, without working yourself into an early grave.

6. Be prepared to make it easy to refer you.

Let them know who you're looking for, describe your ideal client, walk them through how you prioritize your A and B clients, and use the 10 Systems for Client Retention. If you only work with CEOs, tell them that it has to be a high level intro, or it won't work.

Say something like this...

"Jonna, it seems like you guys are growing fast in the IT space, and I bet you do a lot of internal hiring and probably already work with some great firms. Are you open to talking to somebody I think is really great who has helped us out a bunch?"

Don't ask them to work too hard to sell you, or make the intro. Give them an email template so they don't accidentally overdo it.

To:	Joline@goodclients.com
Cc:	Dave.omtopofit@Bestshippingusa.com
Subject:	Good connection for you

Hi Joline,

I wanted to make sure to connect you with Dave Omtopofit. I started working with him about a year ago, and it's been a great help for us. Not sure if there is a mutual fit here, but I thought at a minimum you would want to set up a call with each other. Maybe have Dave come out to tour your plant?

Let me know how else I can help.

Or you could even try something like this: "Hi Jonna, meet Catrin. She has been an amazing resource to us finding great IT talent. You guys are now connected, perhaps start with a phone call, and you may want to invite Catrin out to your office to see what you're doing?"

Very simple. That gets it off the partner's plate fast and sets you up for success with the new client.

REFERRALS FROM PERSONAL CONTACTS, FRIENDS, AND FAMILY

The last category here might be controversial for some of you. Again, this isn't an area you need to necessarily be aggressive around, but I wouldn't ignore it—and stretching out of your comfort zone is the point of this chapter.

My friend Paul once told me that he used to never mix his business and personal life. Not an uncommon thought. Until one day he was at his kid's soccer game, chatting with a fellow parent he saw weekly. The other parent shared with him that he just started working with a great new company and he was planning to send more business their way.

When Paul asked about the company, the parent casually dropped the name of Paul's biggest competitor.

Paul was gutted. For months, he'd had a high-value client standing next to him, and he'd never even thought to have the conversation about what he did for a living. If he had, he would almost certainly have gained another $75,000 in income that year.

Ever since that painful experience, Paul makes sure to follow this simple format with anybody he thinks might end up being a good referral source.

Don't say this...

"Hey friend, I'm always on the hunt for more business. Please think of me whenever you run across some hot prospects." If you've read this far, you already know that isn't the way to phrase it.

Say this instead...

"Jon, you and I go to these soccer games all the time and I hardly get to finish a conversation with you. Would you ever want to grab lunch, or coffee, maybe fill me in more on what you do? I can share what I'm up to, and maybe that leads to us helping each other in some way. Maybe not, but it sounds like fun to me— you interested?"

Now they're either interested in getting together, or they're not. In either case, they're more aware of your professional presence than they ever were. You can also add, "I'll look for you on LinkedIn," as a way to kick off scheduling.

If they ask deeper questions about why you want to get together, just tell them the truth.

For more casual friends/acquaintances…

Say something like this…
"I don't feel like I know you that well, but you seem like a put-together person. I thought it would be cool to learn more about what you do. Maybe I'm able to send clients to you or your firm, or maybe I can become a resource for you in some way. Interested?"

Very low key, but believe me, you have probably had social interactions with dozens of people at this point, if not hundreds, that could have become great clients (as well as better friends!) if you invested a little time in the effort.

For closer friends/relatives...

Say something like this...

"Robert, I've been meaning to ask you more about what you guys do at your company. It seems like whenever we're around each other, that's probably the last thing we want to talk about in detail—so I wondered if you would be up for a lunch or a coffee, where I could find out more about what you do. Maybe I could be a good referral source for you, or who knows—maybe you guys know people my company should be helping. Is that a conversation worth having?"

Again, the vast majority of your close friends and relatives are going to welcome the discussion. It's a win-win-win.

REWARDS, INCENTIVES, AND MOTIVATING YOUR CLIENTS TO CONNECT YOU

The primary reason somebody should refer business to you is because you're really good at what you do, not because you're going to buy them dinner if it happens.

Now, if you *want* to buy somebody dinner after you received a referral, I'm not opposed to that. Just don't make it the primary driver.

If you or your company has a predefined way of thanking people for a referral, you can add it as an afterthought. Don't make it the primary reason for the referral.

Don't say this...

"Sammy, I would really love to earn some referrals from you. In fact, if you can give me some names of people I can call on, I'll give you $250 for each one that turns into a client." I hate how this sounds. I know certain people say this, and it works—but I just don't like the feel, or purpose behind the incentive. It's transactional, not relational.

Say something like this instead...

"Sarah, I'm really enjoying getting to work with you, both personally and professionally. In fact, if there are other people wired like you, with your level of thoughtfulness, it would mean a lot to me if you were open to connecting us. Not sure who that might be, but you're a big part of the reason I do this kind of work. Meeting others like you would be great. Oh, also—if it turns out that you actually do connect us to somebody, my company has this program where they send you to a spa for a day. But don't just do it because of that; I want to meet great people to work with!"

You can still bring it up, just keep it in perspective.

Rewards programs, memberships, client appreciation, and customized gifts or acknowledgements all have value. "An unexpected gift at an unexpected time" often has more power than the promise in advance. If your client loves Vegas, then an awards program that gifts them a trip to Vegas is great. But if you know they enjoy theater, then tickets to a show they've mentioned wanting to see after referring you to a special client will feel so much more personalized.

The relationships with clients that become great close friends are to be cherished and nurtured. If you do it right, the rewards will be unlimited.

I'm guessing during most of this section that you've heard internal pushback about why what I'm suggesting isn't possible, or why it's inappropriate with the clients/communities you call on. That's typical within companies—and even within your own stories you tell yourself. I want to deal with the most common objections that come up all the time, and see if I can help you reconcile what your head is telling you with a possible new reality.

Your Personal Objections to Asking

Everybody wants referrals, and it feels *great* when you get one.

Despite that, most people don't ask for them. Why?

Two reasons.

1. Fear. Good old-fashioned chickening out.
2. It's not a play in the playbook. Too often, it's not rehearsed enough, so we don't try. (I just gave you the playbook, so this one should now be moot.)

Here is a list of internal fears you're likely processing after reading the last section.

1. It seems premature to bring up referrals in the beginning of a relationship. This is probably the most common. Most people I talk to want to wait until after we have "proven" ourselves to the new customer.

Here's the problem: in the beginning of the relationship, when you just got hired, your new customer has high hopes for where this goes. You seem like the best option available in the marketplace, and they really want the relationship to work out.

Realistically, you're trying to help them fix a problem that may be very difficult to fix. It may have been a problem for a long time that can't be fixed quickly—and there is a good chance you discover that your new client is a big part of that problem. Not to mention that almost no project goes perfectly smoothly without incident or wrinkle to iron out. So let me ask you: if you're two months into a project that is more difficult, slightly behind schedule, perhaps slightly over budget, are you more likely to ask for a referral *then* than you were at the smooth-sailing beginning? Of course not.

Also, let's say you wait until the project is completely over, and even if you did a good job, what are the odds that a busy customer will even get back to you at this stage? Often, you can't even get a returned call once the project is wrapped.

At the beginning of the project, right after you were hired, and before you completed any work, is your most effective time to ask for a referral. This is the honeymoon phase, and they're never more likely to recommend you than at that moment. Wait to ask, and it might be too late, after old habits are entrenched.

2. Who are you proving yourself to?

If you took on the client in the first place, obviously you both feel like you were the best option for them. All I'm asking you to do is use one of the multitude of strategies that I brought up early enough to plant the seed.

When you say: "I just wondered if there might be people that you naturally run into that might need this kind of help, and if you would be open to connecting us?" then you've done your job.

They might tell you, "I've already spoken to three people about you that you could help, here is their contact info."

They might say, "I've already told a few people about you; let's see how the project goes."

They might say, "Ask me again at the end of the project." The point is, you're not responsible for their answer; all you're responsible for is inserting this step into your process. If you've done that, you've done all you can.

3. "I just met them, and they just wrote me a check. It feels too pushy."
All of these are just various forms of self-doubt.

You can say *anything* to *anybody* if you say it right. I just gave you lots of examples in this chapter; find 2-3 that appeal to you and get started.

Don't quit before the miracle happens. There is unlimited potential to be unlocked here and built upon. Surround yourself with other like-minded individuals who see the same vision of possibility, and work together to encourage and support each other. If you can't find one, log into our website at *chrisjenningsgroup.com* and sign up for a free program with us to experience what that feels like.

All you need to do at this point is assemble your Personal Referral Plan, which I describe in detail in Chapter Eight. Here's a sample:

Personal Referral Plan

1. Ask every time we go out of our way to do something special
2. Review my onboarding checklist for all my accounts
3. Ask CEO/CXO/COO to get feedback from each account 2 times per year
4. Be the first person to welcome former clients to their new job/company
5. Check the guest list before every lunch and learn at client site & always add 2 more people
6. Build in a referral spot to our invoices/take off sheet/onboarding docs
7. review all Linked-In contacts once per month
8. Gather all my good strategic pertners at our company once per month/quarter
9. Visit 5 clients per month and ask every time
10. Make it clear how hard we work to get it right, and give the customers a referral target

CHRIS
JENNINGS
GROUP
SALES LEADERSHIP & CLIENT RETENTION

Let's get busy and build something special.

## SEVEN

SPECIAL TEAMS AND GETTING THE WHOLE TEAM IN ALIGNMENT

The first time I interviewed Blake, he told me he wasn't "really in sales".

"I'm more of an operations guy," he said.

This was news to me; forty percent of the company's sales were currently running through him. "Okay, but you must be doing something special around here then," I replied.

"Well, it's not really *sales* what I do. Customers call me, or I call them, and I find out what they need, how else I could make their jobs easier. Then I'm able to do things for them because of my industry knowledge and connections. They return the favor by giving me lots of business."

Maybe that doesn't sound like sales to you, or maybe we just need a better name for what Blake described, but that sure sounded like a textbook definition of sales to me.

In their organization, they had a dynamic owner/sales leader named Doug Carpentar, whom everybody loved. Doug was super social, likeable, and he enjoyed getting out and about. He was much more the personality type we think of when we hear "salesperson".

What Blake described, however is actually what we all want from a service provider, and exactly what so many talented Special Teams players already do well. And yet if there isn't good alignment in an organization, the Blakes of the team become a one-off situation, an anomaly instead of a process.

I am here to name this as Special Teams, and give you a process that best utilizes all the fantastically skilled individuals across the organization who would never brand themselves as a salesperson—but the great work they do for your customers, and the sales it leads to, speaks for itself.

In this chapter, you'll learn the following:

- Ideas on how to name and brand your Special Teams effort.
- Examples of other companies and how they successfully align their teams.
- Ideas on how to structure the different groups and their participation levels in the process.
- Recognition and rewards for the Special Teams.

BRANDING YOUR SPECIAL TEAMS PROCESS

Dan and some of his leadership team had seen me speak about Special Teams at a leadership conference. They liked the idea of getting their drivers to help out with customers, so they eagerly went back and told their drivers that they wanted them to help with sales while they were making deliveries, and they would give them $50 every time they got a new customer. Unfortunately for them and their drivers, the idea was not well received. The drivers had no interest in becoming salespeople. Very few bonuses were given out.

It was a little bit like Tom Cruise's attack of genius in *Jerry Maguire*, where he wakes up in the middle of the night with a "great" idea, writes out a manifesto, has it printed in the middle of the night while at a company event, and distributes it to everybody in the company. At first, he's proud and satisfied of his work. Then reality sets in, and he realizes how much he's rocked the boat. He's promptly fired from the company.

How we launch changes in philosophy, process, job responsibilities, or anything new must be branded appropriately and well-thought-out in the delivery of the ask to the impacted parties.

Neither Blake, nor the drivers I just mentioned thought of themselves—or wanted to think of themselves—as a salesperson, at least in the more traditional sense. Yet if any of those people were asked to help with initiatives like...

- Customer Retention
- Customer Expansion
- Customer Loyalty
- Customer Advocacy
- Client Advisor
- Client Expediter
- Client Change Management
- Client Utilization
- New Member Mentorship
- Member Engagement
- Member Information Distributor

...those might be acceptable concepts they could happily get behind.

Here are some additional ways to brand Special Teams roles that better communicates what you're looking for.

- Customer Specialist
- Client Advocate
- Client Educator
- Project Leader
- Project Expert

- Project Expansion Leader
- Project Specialist
- Project Experience Expert
- Facilities Expert
- Construction Site Leader
- Inventory Specialist
- Recruiting & Hiring Manager
- Technology Implementor
- Research Specialist/Manager

All of the above titles carry some weight and authority as to their expertise, and position the Special Teams Groups with the credibility to make meaningful suggestions to clients.

In addition to the titles I've seen utilized effectively, I've also seen clients enroll, assign, and promote people to a designated group of operations with an extra emphasis on broadening, deepening, and expanding the client relationships.

They told me they started an "X" Team assembled to help clients grow with them. This is some internal branding they used (not with clients):

- Special Forces
- Client Deployment Team
- The X Team
- The Accelerators
- The Implementers

- Dream Team
- The Over the Top Club

All of these have potential depending on your company culture. Align the internal and external branding of your Special Teams group to fit what you do for clients, and pick names that will energize your team to reach beyond what they're currently doing,

Here are a couple of case studies to get you thinking.

CASE STUDY #1: GREG AND SAHAR

I recently met with Greg and Sahar, the CEO and VP of Sales & Marketing, to review the progress that implementing this process has made in their organization, and frankly, I was really impressed with their level of intention and focus on implementation. I wasn't surprised, because I found Greg and Sahar to both be really on their game, and interested in action, not just talk.

Greg and I met after I delivered a talk to his Vistage group. He participated actively in the conversation, and it seemed like he was already doing a lot of what I talked about. It turned out that he was a fan of all of the concepts, and knew of many of them, but they weren't being implemented to the level of effect he had hoped for.

He rallied his Vistage members to hire us to repeat the program for several of them and include some of their key managers/market leaders, which we did about a month after I spoke at the Vistage meeting.

Based on the success of that exposure, he asked Sahar and I to bullet out some key ways we could get the program installed and actually happening at his company. We interviewed several key team members to better understand the ins and out of each department; then we built a custom program to be delivered to about 75 of his "Special Teams" Members. The results from that have been outstanding.

Here is what Sahar had to say about 18 months down the road: "We knew we had to brand this appropriately, and for our group we came up with The PXT team (this stands for the Partnership Excellence Team). We invited about 50 of the 75 Special Teams members to participate and set up a rotating leadership schedule with one person being in charge every 6 months. This was a mid-level manager, not upper management. It turned out to be an excellent development tool for us. Every 6 months, the CXO, which we call PXT Leader, takes ownership of the White Glove Client Retention process. It has been amazing."

"That leader takes responsibility for communication across each department to ensure that the customer has the best experience possible. There have been some huge wins as a result:

1. We **saved an account** that could have blown up due to a customer communication error that they made, but we were able to mitigate costs for the client and come up with a very cost effective way to fix the problem that didn't embarrass the client, or throw the whole project into disarray, where they

might have been inclined to throw us under the bus, rather than own it with their leadership.

2. We came up with a **creative solution** to another problem where the customer complained about the durability of our displays. The lead grabbed several members of the PXT team, visited 6-7 of their locations, and quickly came up with a work around of adding handles to the displays so they wouldn't get dragged on the floor and come apart. It not only saved the account, it secured our position with the customer as they were so impressed with the way in which we owned the problem, sent out a task force to fix it, and save the customer thousands of dollars in lost revenue.

3. We recently had great success **improving our vendor relationship** because the PXT lead took ownership of talking to our vendors to come up with creative ideas of how to better serve the customer. A year ago, this never would have happened, yet because of the structure we had in place, and how seriously the lead treats this responsibility, this employee is now considered a "Rising Star" which never would have happened either, if not for the added responsibility, and accountability to her peers across the company.

4. We have had great success getting the **Org Charts filled out**. By adding so many additional names to our database, we have had great success following people to new companies, getting

stickier with our clients leading to more work, and increasing the number of contacts for our CXO to follow up with.

5.   The **Quarterly Business Reviews** have gotten better and better over time. Initially, the sales team really resisted doing these, but they have turned into huge sales tools for us. We do 2 a year at our facility and 2 a year at their facility. We created 10 performance metrics that we review at every QBR. Things like on-time delivery statistics, ways to limit changes that add time and money to the project. It has also helped us get very innovative and creative with the clients, things that nobody else they buy from does. In addition, we have been able to communicate things they can't do, and new things they can start doing with us.

6.   We created a **Post Project Review** process in addition to our Kickoff meeting; it bookends the process. We call out the good, the bad, and the ugly. We learn so much from every client, and they learn from us. We own our part, and coach the client to be more successful with us on every program we run, which has led directly to us running more programs with every client.

7.   We created a "**Destination Model**" with 1-, 3-, and 5-year targets for each client. Client Retention means everything to us.

8. Every month we hold a "**State of the Bay**" meeting where each group is required to report on progress made with each client and we share the results with the whole company.

In summary, Sahar stated, "We show up for our clients. This is a big part of how we run our business, and while some groups internally were slow to come along, eventually, everybody in the company saw what it was doing for us, and everybody got engaged."

Thank you for that, Sahar, and for the amazing work you've done with this!

When I spoke to Greg, the CEO, he echoed much of what Sahar had shared and he added some choice, important commentary.

"The PXT process is a weapon for us. We've become so strong; I wouldn't want to compete against us. We frequently recognize our team and reward their progress. Their work has led to more than a 10% increase in our Net Profits!

In our operations team, our Special Teams focus is our best weapon, and even without individual incentives, everybody is completely bought in. The design of the process is what matters to the team.

Sales is now inspired to go get more business, because they know how great we are operationally. They just keep bringing in new accounts."

Thank you to Greg, Sahar, and the whole PXT team at Bay Cities. Your implementation has been off the charts, and you all have a lot to be proud of.

HOW TO STRUCTURE YOUR TEAM FOR OPTIMAL GROWTH AND PROFITS

Growth is not just about headcount.

Actually, in my opinion, you want the minimum number of people on your sales team complemented by exactly the right amount of project engineers, client advocates, and implementation specialists. Ideally, you should have a minimum of two different Special Teams members assigned to each client in addition to the sales team/account executive.

Each individual will have a different way of influencing the client, as well as offering different insights. Each Special Teams member should be given a specific list of questions that will uncover priorities that the client has—priorities that your company could uniquely handle for them in a way that will improve their lives and your profits, and ideally theirs.

Remember my win-win-win model?

Let's give you some more detail that correlates to the prior examples.

REWARDS, RECOGNITION, AND INCENTIVES

When Dan told me he had given out very few $50 rewards to his drivers, I wasn't surprised. Normally, people in Special Teams roles are used to salary, and perhaps a bonus, but not so much as a commission.

Here are some better options.

1. Promotions with elevated titles, salary, and continued cross training to more broadly serve the organization.
2. Team incentives that include days off with pay, and special events such as trips/sporting events/concert tickets.
3. Recognition with parking spots, car wash services, dinner with a note sent home to the family, and other gifts—get creative.
4. Highlighting accomplishments at companywide meetings, relating specific examples of what was done and specifically how it helped the clients and the company.

You need to make it a primary focus across the organization that this helps all Special Teams members, clients, and the future success of the company. This will lead to new teams being created, additional service offerings, and other processes that serve the customer in a unique way, leading to limitless business opportunities with every customer.

CASE STUDY #2: SCOTT S. CONSTRUCTION COMPANY, SOUTHWESTERN U.S.

I had a great call with a client, Scott, the other day. Scott and his entire team of Project Managers and other key Special Teams players have been working with one of our Senior Coaches and Partner, Anthony Mayo. Anthony is a tremendous individual who gets really deep in the weeds with our customers, and challenges them to improve both personally and professionally. We decided mutually early in the project to consolidate all the Business Development through the Special Teams players and consolidated our workforce to match that effort. Here's what Scott told me:

> We managed to grow our business by about 40% last year, while keeping our headcount the same. Our clients respect us, they like working with us even though we are not the cheapest, and when they leave to go to new companies, they take us with them. Thirty million became fifty million in about a year.
>
> We have been focused on making sure that we get at least an hour of GoLive time each day. Because of this, client communication has been excellent, our referrals are way up, and we're regularly discussing the next project while we're still working the ones we are in, so we can manage our schedule more effectively. We have a much greater awareness because we are following a process.
>
> We don't yet have everybody aligned, but at least 50% of the team has absolute clarity. They're teaching the process to newer people, and we're promoting from within. We don't hire from the industry anymore, because they come with bad habits. We start people in entry level roles, and then coach them up, and promote them. The new people are all completely bought in without the baggage.

We are making more money because we are so focused on the process during the project that our profits keep rising, we have fewer hand offs, and we rely on the Special Teams as the Boots on the Ground to get it right. This is making us much more effective. Nothing is getting lost in translation.

We have clear KPI's that we share with the clients and internally. This is resulting in an increase in repeat business; and most of our clients say it's a privilege to work with us. We have set ourselves apart in the construction community and earned the respect of our customers. We don't like change orders, and we are watching out for our customers so they know what to expect, which is making us operationally sound, and creating huge wins for us and our customers.

On our org charts, we have identified two key Project Managers to share the CXO role. We also have a dedicated QBR practice. All of this has led to a significant increase in referrals. Anthony has been a great mentor, friend, and coach to all of us, and the future is bright, regardless of the economy.

These are Scott's words, not mine. He has been disciplined, open, and dedicated to growing a great workplace where he attracts great talent that want to grow with him. We are honored to have been a small part of his success.

## EIGHT

INDIVIDUAL TOOL KIT AND RESOURCES

If you've made it this far in the book, and you're in an individual production or Special Teams role, then pay close attention. In this chapter, I'll share with you some tools that will make this journey easier. These tools are all designed to make these concepts a living, breathing system that resides in your being, based on a commitment to implement the strategies in a relatable way in your company and your life.

Here's the deal: I want you to promise me—and more importantly, yourself—that you will teach these tools to somebody else who could also use them. There are a ton of free resources to download at *chris jenningsgroup.com*; they don't even have to buy anything. If you read my first book, you know I am huge in investing in yourself. What better investment could there be?

These are the five tools you'll learn in this section:

1. Trail Map for Client Retention
2. Individual Goals and Corresponding Goal Board
3. Your personal 30 Minute Success Plan
4. Referral Plan and Playbook
5. Self-Accountability Tracker/Scorecard

TRAIL MAP FOR CLIENT RETENTION

If you haven't already, download this tool from *chrisjenningsgroup. com*. All the concepts I've shared with you in this book are summarized with visual cues for you to work this into your daily life. Think of it like the playbook that quarterbacks have on their wrists. It's a quick reference guide to all the tools. Put your goals in the middle of it and reference it every day.

It will likely take you at least 90 days, and potentially an entire year, to weave these into your consciousness. Once you do, though, you will be getting more done, more easily, in much less time. Invest 30-90 mins per week on this now, and you'll save yourself countless hours of struggles with clients and team members down the road.

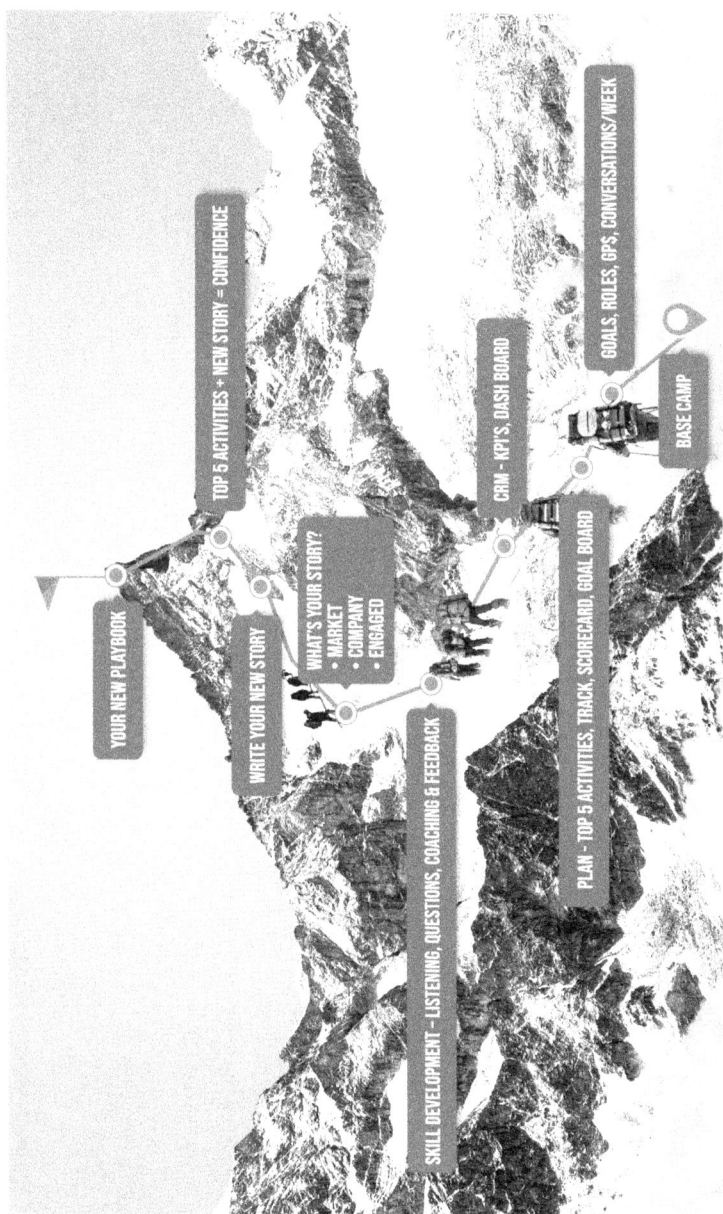

YOUR NEW PLAYBOOK

TOP 5 ACTIVITIES + NEW STORY = CONFIDENCE

WRITE YOUR NEW STORY

WHAT'S YOUR STORY?
• MARKET
• COMPANY
• ENGAGED

SKILL DEVELOPMENT – LISTENING, QUESTIONS, COACHING & FEEDBACK

CRM – KPI'S, DASH BOARD

PLAN – TOP 5 ACTIVITIES, TRACK, SCORECARD, GOAL BOARD

GOALS, ROLES, GPS, CONVERSATIONS/WEEK

BASE CAMP

Conversations Made Easy

Before you go

Expectations

Unique Connections

Set An Agenda

Explore Their World

Find: Time/$/Resources

Understand Who Cares

Let Them Know You

How Big is the Problem?

Hours

Emotions

Adversity

Relationships

Dollars

Goals

Business

Roles:

KPI's:

Results:

Personal

1.

2.

3.

4.

5.

Best 5 Questions To Ask

1.

2.

3.

4.

5.

N ext Steps

O nboarding

W hat Else Can We Do/Referrals

☎ **949-463-5755**
🌐 **www.chrisjenningsgroup.com**
✉ chris@chrisjenningsgroup.com

Client Retention Matrix

1. Go Live & Special Teams

2. New Client on Boarding

3. Customer Org Chart

4. Quarterly Business Review

5. Update Customer Goals

6. Clear Hand Offs

7. Define Top 5 Client Qualities

8. Who is the CXO?

9. Customer Targets & Renewals

10. Referrals to your Customers

What's Your Story?

Personal

1.

2.

3.

Business

1.

2.

3.

I encourage you to take a photo of your Trail Map and post it on LinkedIn. Share the tool with your clients and team members to let them know how effective it is in helping you to help them.

Update your scores on the 10 Systems every 90 days and watch the results follow the scores up or down.

INDIVIDUAL GOALS AND GOAL BOARDS

Maybe you decided to pick up this book on your own, or maybe somebody "suggested" it to you as a team building exercise. In either case, this has to *matter* to you. If it doesn't, stop reading. I am pretty well convinced that most individuals and companies could use the material included here; that's my experience to date. However, this is for people who need it and want it, not for people who are just going through the motions. I know you could double your results, but what's more important is that *you* know you could double your results.

To that end, I think you need to pick some goals that drive you.

If you're in a personal production/sales role. The 3 most important goals you can set for yourself are usually:

1. An income target
2. Gross Profit dollars required to achieve that income target
3. Number of new and existing client appointments needed per week to achieve Goals 1 and 2

If you are a Key Special Teams member, not attached to a revenue target, your three most important business goals might look different. They could be any of the following:

1. Go on three Quarterly Business Reviews/month
2. Walk one client factory floor/per month
3. Attend two new client/project onboarding sessions per week
4. Call five clients a month for a "Feedback" session

Choose the goals that are relevant for your situation, then share them with your team. The corresponding salesperson, the Head of Ops, and ultimately the customer.

Now, as for building your personal goals and tying them to your professional goals, make it your mission to get a goal board up and renew it every year.

If you have never assembled a goal board/vision board/dream board, they go by lots of names, there is a chance you are selling yourself short in this pass through life. This is a chance to fight the outside world's programming of what you believe you are entitled to, and walk, run, or sprint to another possible existence.

The goal board is a large piece of white cardboard, upon which you place pictures of what you want to have happen in your life. Many people do a digital version of the goal board using images they pull from Pinterest or Google. However you choose to create it, the important thing again here is that you actually do so.

Don't think about it: *do it*. Do it tonight. Invite your friends to join you; share it with your family, people you live with, people you work with. Do it as a team meeting. Do it with your children; teach your children and their friends how to build a brighter future than their present.

Pictured below is a beautiful example of one goal board. Our dear friend Lisa, whose kids regularly make goal boards and share them with us. We reward them with $50 every time they share their goals and dreams with us.

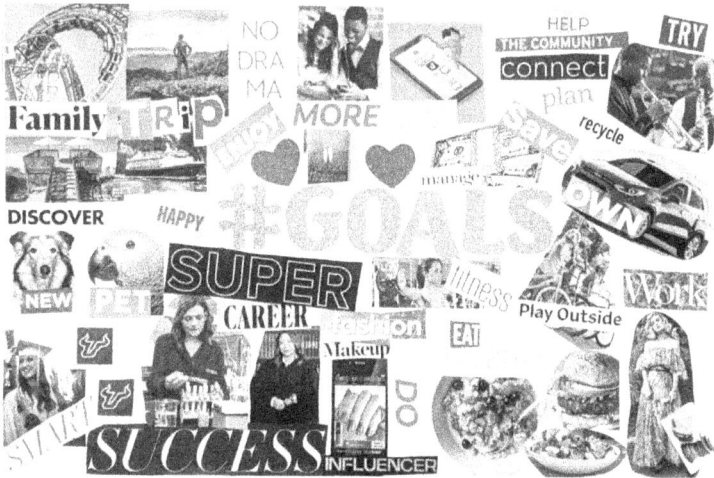

My kids, who are all in their thirties and older now, still get the same deal. I am interested in their lives. $50 seems a small price to pay to help somebody else build a brighter future.

In professional settings, picture the world you are trying to create, and select a photo or several photos/drawings/billboard messages that encapsulate that. Get your subconscious working for you, not against you. Take some responsibility for programming where your mind goes.

I have never had anybody who created a vision board tell me this wasn't worth doing. I have had several people come back and tell me that they have accomplished everything—yes, everything—that they put on their board. Try it! Open your mind to the possibilities, and see where it takes you. Now, remember, you have to back up the dreams with the work. This brings us to....

PERSONAL PLAN

If you are in a full time sales/personal production role, your personal plan will be a bit longer. If you are a critical Special Teams member with limited time for customer GoLive dialogue, then your personal plan will be modified to fit your role.

Full Time Sales/Business Development/Personal Production
Recall your top 3 goals that you developed previously. Then create an activity list of at least five specific actions you are going to take to hit all of your goals. Now, I went through an extensive list of activities and how to best perform those activities in my first book, *Conversations Made Easy*, so you can review the "Do Something" section in that book as needed.

I call this a 30 Minute Success Plan. You'll take 30 minutes to get your ideas down on paper, then hold yourself accountable to do those activities. For full time Sales roles, it might look like this:

CHRIS
JENNINGS
GROUP

Name: _____

30 Minute Plan - Success Plan

GOALS

Income: $ _____ Yr

Sales: $ _____ Yr

Appointments: _____ Wk

ACTIVITIES	Goal
1) Referrals/Introductions	2 per wk
2) Client lunch & learn	1 per mo
3) New Product Demo	1 per wk
4)	
5)	
6)	
7)	
8)	
9)	
10)	

You can find blank and completed examples on *chrisjenningsgroup.com*.

Now, for Special Teams players, your situations are unique, and therefore your plans are unique. It's really about thinking through the issues I suggested earlier. Ask yourself these questions:

1. What opportunities are easy for me to see, or hear about given my role?
2. What could I point out to customers that would help them the most?
3. What's the easiest way I can think of to enter into a conversation with a customer to address questions 1 and 2?

Once you've thought through those answers, come up with your activities. For example:

If you're a driver for a Seafood Company...

1. Always ask the Chef/Manager/Server: what's selling these days, and why?
2. How many stars are they getting on Yelp?
3. Offer to have one of your company Chefs host an event at your restaurant and publicize it for more traffic.

If you're a Project Manager for a kitchen and bath remodeler...

1. Always ask the homeowner about their wish list of projects to do "someday."

2. Meet with them as they're moving out to walk through a "potential change order" checklist.
3. Walk through the add-ons that might have been over looked in the effort to finish designing the project.

If you're on the support desk for a technology company...

1. Ask the customers: when they originally bought the technology, what was their primary motivator?
2. Offer a quick review of the different levels of care plans to make sure they are on the most cost effective, and helpful plan.
3. Ask them: what are the three other technologies they count on the most? See if there might not be smart recommendations you could make.

Remember, the Special Teams players have a much lower credibility hurdle to overcome, and you probably can help the customers by being very direct when they aren't utilizing the right blend of products and services you offer.

CASE STUDY: "I DIDN'T KNOW YOU DID THAT"

Our client, Rene Ruiz, was attending a program at our office in Irvine, California. We were rolling out the Client Retention Matrix for their entire Special Teams groups, which consisted of the vast majority of their total head count. After sharing the significance of "what else we do" with their team, Rene felt compelled to share a story of his own.

He told us, "I was visiting with a client last week who we've had for almost thirty years. We do a ton of work with them; about $3 million per year. While I was there, my main contact, Robin—who loves me, by the way—made an offhanded reference to an event she was attending the next week with their sister division. It turned out that they have an entire division that runs off its own P&L and does the same work under a different brand. So, for the past twenty-eight years, I could have been doing another $3 million a year with that sister division! I nearly had a heart attack on the spot. Boy, do I wish I had met you then!"

Get with your team and get your KPIs lined up for each Special Teams role in the company. Remember, anybody who talks to customers is a Special Teams member. Utilize them the right way, and better connect to your customers.

REFERRAL PLAN AND PLAYBOOK

Referrals are the best way to get business; they're the quickest to close, with the best margins, and the least amount of competition. Build a referral plan for each Special Teams player, and follow the trail to your goals.

Have each team member ask: what are the top 3-5 things I can do to generate those referrals?

Going back to our prior examples, the driver at the Seafood company could:

1. Ask who are the new restaurants in town that people are talking about, then follow up by asking: are you friendly with them?
2. When offering to bring their internal Chefs in to do some recipe sharing ideas, see if they want to invite guests such as other vendors, or perhaps even customers. All of the other invitees become potential referral sources.
3. Ask "If I ever had leftover fresh fish left on my route, where would be a good place to bring it?"

Get creative, get a plan, get good at referrals.

The Project Manager at the Kitchen and Bath remodeler could:

1. Ask how it's going with the neighbors during the project, and see if they were hosting a block party to show off their

new kitchen to their friends. The homeowner inviting neighbors, friends, and family creates a natural referral environment.

2. Maybe you offer to hire a high-quality chef to cook in their new kitchen; that could be a cross-promotion for both of you.

3. Maybe you work with a local realtor to show off your new kitchen and give them ideas for their buyers coming into the neighborhood. This could inspire the realtor to send you more business and become a key strategic partner and referring partner.

The Technical Support/Help Desk could:

1. Enroll their customers in training on your products and invite your customers to invite guests.

2. Ask the customers if *their* customers need this kind of software too, and if it would help them if more of their customers used the same technology.

3. Show them an extra cool hack or short cut your technology offers, and then ask them to teach that to others in or outside of their company. Follow up immediately with, "So, who are you going to teach this to?"

There are a million options in creating the referral plan. Pick the ones that work for you and get rolling!

SELF-ACCOUNTABILITY

We just spent several pages reviewing these rules and strategies, and now it's time for you to put them to work. Maybe you want to run the company you work at, or maybe you want to stay in your role and be great. In either case, you now need to establish tools and strategies, so this information doesn't fly out of your head like the thing you were looking for when you went downstairs, and then only remembered when you were upstairs again.

Here are five simple practices to keep you on track:

1. Tell five people your plan.
2. Get a scorecard going now.
3. Put money on it! Give your friend, colleague, roommate, or other handy individual $100.
4. Trigger a contest with co-workers or strategic partners.
5. Get an accountability group and/or coach outside of your company and family.

Tell Five People Your Plan

The more you make your goals public, the more you will stick to your word. Self-accountability requires some crazy discipline; but public accountability is much easier to follow through with. For example, if you tell your friend Tom that you're going to meet him every Monday night on the tennis court at 8 pm, then even if you are dog-tired at 7:45, and really don't want to play, odds are high you drag yourself out to the court. And while you are out there, you start to feel really good because you followed through and did what you said you were going to do.

Without public accountability, then you might go down the excuse path. That just sucks, because you start buying into your own nonsense, creating headline news about how this was a bad idea. You end up shortchanging yourself and live less of a life than you imagined. If this were easy, everybody would do it. You want there to be some degree of difficulty. Work your way through it and leave your less engaged competitors in the dust.

Get a Scorecard Going Now

This simple tool is just a tracking device that gives you a physical, mental, and emotional reason to keep going, versus quitting before the miracle happens.

Please see the example below, and feel free to download off our website *chrisjenningsgroup.com*.

Get it ingrained in your day to day and week to week. Eventually, everything I am suggesting you do will come from muscle memory, and it will feel relatively easy. Like I just said, you want this to be hard enough to keep you in elite performance territory, simply because of the new habits and commitments you are making.

While this section specifically refers to your own self-accountability, getting more people around you doing this will also reinforce the habit.

Activities Scorecard

Month: _____   **This Week's Date:** Monday _____ to Friday _____

SCORECARD INSTRUCTIONS: *1. Set your weekly goal and plan your cold calling activities in your calendar, and don't cancel! 2. Record your results daily.*

MON.	TUES.	WED.	THURS.	FRI.
# GO LIVE ____	# GO LIVE ____	# GO LIVE ____	# GO LIVE ____	# GO LIVE ____
# CLIENT ENT ____	# CLIENT ENT ____	# CLIENT ENT ____	# CLIENT ENT ____	# CLIENT ENT ____
# CALLS MADE ____	# CALLS MADE ____	# CALLS MADE ____	# CALLS MADE ____	# CALLS MADE ____
# NETWORKING ____	# NETWORKING ____	# NETWORKING ____	# NETWORKING ____	# NETWORKING ____
#LNL//ZOOMINAR ____	#LNL//ZOOMINAR ____	#LNL//ZOOMINAR ____	#LNL//ZOOMINAR ____	#LNL//ZOOMINAR ____
OTHER: ____				
#OF CALLS COMPLETED	#OF CALLS COMPLETED	#OF CALLS COMPLETED	#OF CALLS COMPLETED	#OF CALLS COMPLETED
1 2 3 4 5	1 2 3 4 5	1 2 3 4 5	1 2 3 4 5	1 2 3 4 5
6 7 8 9 10	6 7 8 9 10	6 7 8 9 10	6 7 8 9 10	6 7 8 9 10
11 12 13 14 15	11 12 13 14 15	11 12 13 14 15	11 12 13 14 15	11 12 13 14 15
# OF DECISION MAKERS CONTACTED	# OF DECISION MAKERS CONTACTED	# OF DECISION MAKERS CONTACTED	# OF DECISION MAKERS CONTACTED	# OF DECISION MAKERS CONTACTED
1 2 3 4 5	1 2 3 4 5	1 2 3 4 5	1 2 3 4 5	1 2 3 4 5
6 7 8 9 10	6 7 8 9 10	6 7 8 9 10	6 7 8 9 10	6 7 8 9 10
# OF APPOINTMENTS SET	# OF APPOINTMENTS SET	# OF APPOINTMENTS SET	# OF APPOINTMENTS SET	# OF APPOINTMENTS SET
1 2 3 4 5	1 2 3 4 5	1 2 3 4 5	1 2 3 4 5	1 2 3 4 5
# OF REFERRALS	# OF REFERRALS	# OF REFERRALS	# OF REFERRALS	# OF REFERRALS
1 2 3 4 5	1 2 3 4 5	1 2 3 4 5	1 2 3 4 5	1 2 3 4 5

List New Appointments/ Name of Prospective Customer	Next Step Date - Date Of Appointment	Scale of 1-10	Briefly Describe Why This Is A Qualified Prospect	Born On Date
1.				
2.				
3.				
4.				
5.				
6.				
7.				
8.				
9.				
10.				

TOTALS: # of New Appointments: _____   # of New Appointments MTD: _____

Color code them. Do something creative with them, that boring old Chris Jennings didn't think of, and post the suggestion on our website, LinkedIn, or YouTube channel.

Give Your Colleague, Friend, Or Other Handy Individual $100

It adds a little extra zing when there is actual money on the line. Make an agreement with somebody, or a group of somebodies, that want to do the same thing you want to do—or anything else that they want to do that is of equivalent degree of difficulty or less. Yes, or less. If they want to climb Everest once a week, we already know that is not happening, but if they want to say a prayer every day, we know they could for sure do that, and just the mere act of identifying the activities, that you both, or all want to follow through on, you are way ahead.

It's not much different, but it adds some spice. It keeps it interesting, and in some ways adds gamification to the process, which only makes you stronger, and it gives you a chance to teach the concept to others, which only makes you stronger. Good all the way around as far as I am concerned. Have them, or a neutral 3rd party hold the $100 bill, and show it to you each week you stick to your commitment, or deposit/spend it if you don't. I don't care how much money you have, you probably won't miss more than a week a year.

Initiate a Contest with Coworkers and/or Strategic Partners

Find a group somewhere that likes to compete. Come up with appropriate first, second, and third place prizes. Track it publicly and get really productive.

Have some fun with this! Get some teams involved, name them, get matching shirts, rally the team members to get involved. The more obscure, and different the new activity feels, the more you are going to have to work at this. The example below is of a "Bingo" game that we created at a client offsite. Every time an individual ran a string of

Name _____

Date _____   Q1 Q2 Q3 Q4

	B	I	N	G	O
Referral					
Upsell					
Expedite $					
CXO Call					
QBR					

CHRIS
JENNINGS
GROUP

Name _____

Date _____   Q1 Q2 Q3 Q4

	B	I	N	G	O
Referral	////	////			
Upsell	////	////			
Expedite $	////				
CXO Call	////				
QBR	////	////			

CHRIS
JENNINGS
GROUP

5 in a row, they screamed Bingo, and were celebrated company wide. Adding some cool gifts behind it makes it even more fun.

Get behind this and see what happens. If it doesn't feel like you, do one of the other suggestions or create something different and tell us about it.

Assemble an Accountability Group, and/or Hire a Coach

Just because your company isn't motivating you the way you like to be motivated, or they are stretched too thin with internal resources, or whatever the circumstances might be, none of those are reasons to not get busy with what I am describing. I understand it may be harder, but as you may have heard me say before: **The hard thing to do, and the right thing to do, are probably the same.**

You don't have the help you need where you work? Hire a coach. Maybe the company reimburses you, maybe not? It doesn't matter. This is your career. Your life. Your future. Own it. Get it done. Don't wait.

Assemble a group of peers, friends, strategic partners. Download some of our videos at *chrisjenningsgroup.com*. Watch them independently, and then get with your group and discuss. Hire one of our coaches, or pass this info on to your coach, and ask them to interpret for your situation.

If you haven't noticed, we just want to help you get better. I sincerely hope you want that for yourself, and you do the things required to get there.

If you made it this far, and you are in a personal production role and don't currently manage a team, or have any desire to ever manage a team, you might be done.

If you have people around you who count on you to help a group get more done, keep reading and I will give you a few more suggestions to make your whole organization profitable, engaged, and growing well beyond what you originally imagined.

## NINE

LEADERSHIP TOOL KIT

In this book, I've given you a bunch of tools, ideas, and suggestions to help individuals and teams grow. It's every leader's job to look smartly at their organization and see what they can do to help improve the lives and opportunities for their company, team members, and other groups.

In this chapter, I'll lay out six remaining items that will help you lead your team to grow, both personally, and professionally.

1. Trail Map for Client Retention
2. Creating your own Client Retention Matrix/Playbook

3. Calculating your True Cost of Sales
4. Assessing Talent and Asking the Right Ask
5. Referral Madness
6. Compensation for Customers and Your Team

TRAIL MAP FOR CLIENT RETENTION

Earlier in this read, I recommended going to *chrisjenningsgroup.com* and downloading the Client Retention Trail Map; if you haven't done that, please do it now. This tool is made for you and your team members to gain phenomenal clarity on what you want the team to do. It helps remind each Special Teams member or other team members about their Why: why they're doing this and what result they hope it leads to. I am certain this will be in an electronic format at some point, but in the meantime, and forever, I hope you pull this out and scribble away with what all this means to you!

The Trail Map for Client Retention will probably mean something different to each person who uses it, and it might evolve, change, and take on completely different meanings as you and the organization evolve. There is a framework provided for you for almost everything I have written about, and I am confident we have video resources that better clarify the purpose, message, and practical how-to's to make this easier to implement. Let's roll!

As an aside, I often use the phrase "let's roll" when I want to highlight something important. If you don't already recognize its origin, let me take a moment to explain.

We all remember the international tragedies that occurred on US soil and airspace on September 11th, 2001. Perhaps the most compelling story was conveyed through cell phone communications while it was happening. A group of passengers, who thanks to those cell communications now had awareness of what their hijackers were about to do, decided to re-take the plane, even though they would likely lose their lives in the process. The last recording of their voices, where they were explaining their plan to loved ones, ended with passenger Todd Beamer's voice saying, "Let's roll."

I don't bring this up to be dramatic; I bring it up to put life in perspective. Ironically, I am on a flight right now as I write this. God willing, I will land safely at home tonight, and hug my wife when I arrive home and tell her that I love her. The fact that so many people lost their lives that day, including those on United 93, should make us all insanely grateful for the mundane, somewhat ordinary tasks that we all "get" to do, not "got" to do. So, perhaps take a moment in silent prayer or reflection of what life has afforded us, and allow that to be one piece of motivation that helps you lead others to an even better life. As far as I know, we only get one time through here on Earth. Let's make it an incredible experience for us, and all the people around us.

Encourage people to play around with the format. Customize it to fit your individual organization, or team. Get the Trail Maps dirty. Overused. Use them until they fit you and your organization like a comfortable old pair of jeans. Then you will know you are doing most, if not all, of the right things.

The Goals/Roles/KPIs in the center, are for sure going to be different from person to person. Review them regularly. Have your team share them broadly with other colleagues, even clients, to show the significance of the effort.

Take the example of what Joel, who works at the Ritz Carlton, did when my dear friend Les asked him to review their "12 Service Values" document when we were at brunch one day. Joel had it with him, he pulled it out and shared the Value that was covered that morning. He shows up to work, to excel at work, and at home, every day, incorporating those values into his work and personal life.

If you didn't know this, the Ritz Carlton lives and breathes 12 Service Values. In fact, they are so important to the organization, that they hold a daily stand up meeting and review 1 of the 12 values every day before the team takes the floor.

These systems start with great leadership, and our job as leaders is to set the tone for the team around us, and help them achieve more *with* us, not *for* us.

CREATE YOUR CUSTOM CLIENT RETENTION MATRIX PLAYBOOK

I've read a lot of books with good ideas. Some of my favorites have included some really cool tools—which have helped me create my own.

One phenomenal read is *The Five Love Languages* by Gary Chapman. It's great, very simple material that has stuck with me—but it is also so easy to forget, and I often find myself wishing I had a portable cheat sheet to keep with me at all times. I was on a road trip with some buddies this weekend, and we spent a good amount of time discussing the principles from this book; that cheat sheet would have come in handy. The Custom Client Retention Matrix Playbook is that cheat sheet for this book.

Across the top, I want you to write in all the different Special Teams groups that exist in your organization. Down the lefthand side is all 10 systems with your scores as you see them today.

The playbook allows you to prioritize which special teams group needs the most attention with which Client Retention System. You can use either check boxes to highlight, or you can get granular and score each box as you see it today to help you prioritize and create a prioritization list.

As I mentioned earlier, this is not going to be a fix where everything is done overnight, even if you hired us to implement it. There is likely to be some plodding along and trial and error to get it going. Set goals. If you start the year at 41, try to get to 71 by the end of year 1, and 81 by the end of year 2. If you can get there, you have clearly created a world-class team, implementing world-class systems, with incredible payoff for all.

Special Teams

TOTALS

The Client Retention Matrix

Name: _____   Date: _____

1. Go Live & Special Teams
2. New Client On Boarding
3. Customer Org Chart
4. Quarterly Business Review
5. Update Customer Goals
6. Clear Hand Offs
7. Define Top 5 Clients
8. Who is the CXO?
   Contract Renewal and
9. Setting Customer Targets
10. Referrals To Your Customers

Total

CHRIS JENNINGS GROUP

chris@chrisjenningsgroup.com | www.chrisjenningsgroup.com | 949-463-5755

CHRIS JENNINGS GROUP

chris@chrisjenningsgroup.com | www.chrisjenningsgroup.com | 949-463-5755

The Client Retention Matrix

Name: XYZ Inc. Date: 10-25-23

Special Teams

	Go Live & Special Teams	New Member On-boarding	Customer org Chart	Quarterly Business Reviews	Update Customer Goals	Clear Hand Offs	Define Top 5 Clients	Who is CXO?	Contract Renewal and Setting Customer Targets	Referrals To Your Customers	Total
(count)	4	6	3	3	5	5	2	1	6	3	38
Project Management	11/30	12/31	11/30								
Field Supervisor					12/31						
Engineering				3/30							
Tech Support						12/31					
Exec Line									2/28		
Install									1/31		
Accounting											
TOTALS											

Goal 68 by 1/31

chris@chrisjennings-group.com www.chrisjennings-group.com 949 450 1425

CHRIS JENNINGS GROUP

CALCULATING YOUR TRUECOST OF SALES

You know I root for all sales teams to succeed and bring a ton to the table for the organization and the customers they serve. I will also say that if they aren't doing the work, and not getting the GoLive time they need to do great work, then you can still lead the organization to the top by having an incredible Special Teams group. In fact, with a well-coached Special Teams group, you can make the most of every opportunity with or without a Sales team around them.

TRUECOST of sales & going to market
** Please fill in the following to the best of your ability

CHRIS
JENNINGS
GROUP

Sales Team Salary & Employment Costs: Salary/Commission/Bonus_____ + Employment Costs_____ = **Total:**_____

CSR Team: Salary/Commission/Bonus_____ + Employment Costs_____ = **Total:**_____

% of All other customer facing employees'__ Salary/Commission Bonus_____ + Employment Costs_____ = **Total:**_____

Lead costs (Website/marketing/advertising/trade show/Events)_____   **Total:**_____

Hidden production costs (wasted inventory/downtime/setup fees)_____   **Total:**_____

Fluctuating inventory value/spoilage/waste_____   **Total:**_____

Lost production due to lost opportunities (Conversion rate x Hours + Effort + expenses)_____   **Total:**_____

Other:_____   **Total:**_____

Other:_____   **Total:**_____

Estimated total TRUECOST of sales: **Total:**_____

Total TRUECOST sales_____/Total Revenue_____ = Total TRUECOST %_____ **12-month Target/ Goal**

Current Gross Profit %_____ - Current TRUECOST %_____ = Profit Differential_____ **12-month Target**

Don't get me wrong; I've seen many examples of this system working extremely well with *both* groups. But you should remember to manage your costs appropriately. If you're investing in a sales team, let's make sure they're a highly productive sales team.

Once again, these are available as a download on our website.

TRUECOST of sales & going to market
** Please fill in the following to the best of your ability

CHRIS
JENNINGS
GROUP

Sales Team Salary & Employment Costs: Salary/Commission/Bonus 1.0 M + Employment Costs .3 M = Total: 1.3 M

CSR Team: Salary/Commission/Bonus .2 M + Employment Costs .06 M = Total: .26 M

% of All other customer facing employees' Salary/Commission Bonus .4 M + Employment Costs .12 M = Total: .52 M

Lead costs (Website/marketing/advertising/trade show/Events) 1.0 M Total: 1.0 M

Hidden production costs (wasted inventory/downtime/setup fees) .75 M Total: .75 M

Fluctuating inventory value/spoilage/waste .25 M Total: .25 M

Lost production due to lost opportunities (Conversion rate x Hours + Effort + expenses) .5 M Total: .5 M

Other: Total:

Other: Total:

Estimated total TRUECOST of sales: Total: 4.58 M

Total TRUECOST sales 4.58 M/Total Revenue 10.0 M = Total TRUECOST % 45.8 **12-month Target/ Goal** 35.8%

Current Gross Profit % .50 - Current TRUECOST % 45.5 = Profit Differential 4.2% **12-month Target** 14.2%

Sit with your CFO and calculate your costs. Maybe there is a way to reallocate funds to help grow your sales, and grow it more profitably—which can only help the whole team.

Often, lots of dollars get thrown at the sales effort—some of which has great payback, some not as much. My bottom line for you is to grow your *organizational* bottom line while you grow and develop the systems and skills of your team. Win win win!

You win. Your team wins. Your customer wins.

This is how it needs to be, and if you work towards it, buy into the process, and work the process, it's all there for you.

ASSESSING TALENT AND ASKING THE RIGHT ASK

Rudy and Sylvo are both Project Managers at the same company. They both have been asked to take an active interest in retaining and growing clients. Rudy has a huge desire to do more in this arena; Sylvo does not. Sylvo is a great worker, as is Rudy—they just have similar roles with different goals. We need to accommodate for the strengths, weaknesses, and desires that come with both.

As human beings, we all operate differently. I am a huge fan of identifying the best way there for each individual based on what the four sciences, detailed in the next section, tell us.

If you read my first book, *Conversations Made Easy: Building Your*

Playbook for Growing Sales & Connecting with Customers, you'll recognize this next part.

System # 9: Unbiased Assessment Tools

Before starting in the field I now work in, on my way out of a role that felt very unsatisfying, I completed a personality profile to lead me to a more fulfilling career. Included as one of the suggestions was that I consider becoming a poultry scientist. I didn't know that was an option; I passed on that.

Another assessment tool that I used suggested that I have no business being in sales at all based on my acquired skills. My extraordinarily low income that year, chronicled much earlier in that book, might have seemed to justify that assertion, but I was passionate about what I started. I saw glimpses of where my future successes could lie, and I was relentlessly dedicated to the process.

So, the fact that I sit here today ready to suggest to you that there are assessment tools based in real behavioral science that are worth exploring may seem puzzling to you. I have worked hard to keep an open mind and become a lifelong learner, which keeps life interesting and hopefully slows down the aging process.

The reasons I rely on and use these specific tools are twofold:

1. I have spoken in great detail about the trends and common observations I have made over decades in the field. However,

THE CLIENT RETENTION MATRIX

individual coaching must be tailored to the individual. We are all created equal, but we are not all created the same. Knowing the tendencies in our personal profiles helps us create a path to improved performance and significantly improves our communication skills. This is often critical for those who relied on their technical expertise and gave less energy to how they communicated.

2. If I am trying to match somebody to a new role in **Special Teams**, having some third-party objective feedback that doesn't have anything to do with what schools we went to or what similar backgrounds we had, but is just purely a data-driven indication of what would come more easily to one person than another also just makes sense. Yes, I could be a good corporate citizen and follow protocols, but there was a lot in me from the beginning that could indicate to a prospective employer about how much work it would take to get me productive, and if somebody wanted to hire me, giving them a what to do and what not to do scenario on me, would be an overwhelmingly positive thing to do for everybody involved.

After years of experimenting with different tools and behavioral sciences, here are the four methods I lean on to accomplish the objectives.

First Behavioral Science: DISC

Odds are, at this point in your career, you have taken a **DISC** profile. Although, there are several **DISC** providers who repackage the advice in a myriad of ways. Not all are created equal.

DISC divides the world into quadrants, where each one of us has a primary behavioral style and secondary behavioral style. We tend to follow those styles in all areas of our lives, and those tendencies are not likely to vary unless, perhaps, we are under intense pressure. Even under pressure, many of us don't deviate from our natural style; the more we deviate from our natural **DISC** style in our communication, the more stress is created in our life. It takes a lot of thought and energy to have multiple modalities in our hip pocket for dealing with life on life's terms.

Below are the four DISC styles.

- D—**Drivers** tend to be direct, willing to take risks, less concerned with feelings or detail, focused on a goal, and moving fast. **Animal reference—The Lion.**

- I—**Influencers** tend to be moving fast, risk takers, big picture, talkative, and really enjoy the spotlight. **Animal reference— The Dolphin.**

- S—**Socializers** tend to be friendly, empathetic, inclusive, risk-averse, slower, interested in people more than process. **Animal Reference—The Labrador.**

- **C—Analyticals** tend to be scientific, careful, and cautious, detailed and slower, exacting, and prioritizing process over people, very risk-averse. **Animal Reference—The Owl.**

None of these are right or wrong, just different ways of prioritizing how to communicate in the world. (Note, if you are high D, you probably think everybody who doesn't see the world like you do is wrong.)

Understanding DISC and how to alter your approach from what feels most natural to you to what is the best way for your audience will help professionally in two ways. (This will help anyone at home too.)

1. Your team: why does Johnny feel the need to go over so much detail? Their **DISC** profile can probably answer that for you. We recommend having your **DISC** profile in your email signature or outside your office to give the world a fighting chance to tailor their message to you in the best way possible.

2. Your customers: wouldn't it be easier, and I love things to be easier, if instead of being a one-size-fits-all robot, you found a way to tailor your presentation and entire customer experience to the way your customer communicates?

All that for the first science.

Second Behavioral Science: Motivators and Driving Forces

We all have motivational tendencies that guide us. Certainly, it would be good to know if you are more motivated by being in charge and getting it done on your own or by collaborating with a big group.

Or, understanding if you want to make judgments based on your instincts or by doing more research.

There are twelve Motivational Profiles:

- Resourceful vs. Selfless
- Objective vs. Harmonious
- Collaborative vs. Commanding
- Intentional vs. Altruistic
- Receptive vs. Structured
- Intellectual vs. Instinctive

Once we know our profiles for our teams, we can use or avoid specific language just based on this. We can help people pick the right roles for themselves rather than put them in situations that might work against them. Ultimately, I think we are all happiest when we are surrounded by a supportive culture that has similar values and clearly understands the reasons for somebody having different priorities.

Take a guess where you fit, and perhaps take another look at it after you complete the assessments.

Third Behavioral Science: Learned Skills and Competencies

We have identified twenty-five basic skills that will help people make great salespeople, leaders, and a multitude of other roles in the world.

For the purposes of this read, I am referencing how to use these tools for customer-facing roles, but I have helped organizations hire CEOs, investment personnel, project managers, and many other roles. The best executive recruiters use these tools to help them make the right choice, put the right person in the right role, and help new hires get up to speed more quickly than anyone would without the feedback in the assessment.

Fourth Behavioral Science: EQ (Emotional Intelligence)

I could have made the whole book about EQ.

It's a really smart way to look at our ability to read and regulate emotion. Understanding our emotional state, being able to read the emotional state of the room, and then adjusting ours to meet that of our audience are absolute musts.

EQ measures that as well as our motivational state. Life in sales is filled with highs and lows and a preponderance of things "not going our way."

If you are engaged in the process of what you do, are not overly attached to the outcome, and are convinced you have something super useful to offer, your motivation should come from that source and not be overly dependent on the results.

We need to continue to learn from our "losses," and turn losses into lessons that make us better equipped to help the next individual we encounter.

Several books are written on emotional intelligence, and we have built multiple coaching sessions that you can download or participate in to learn more about this topic—all available at *chrisjenningsgroup.com*.

All too often, many in sales feel the need to create a wall around themselves, so they don't feel the hurt of things not going their way. The downside is that you are then walled off from multiple emotional cues and clues that are needed and could be put to good use.

You want your prospect or customer to feel that you truly "get them."

There cannot be any disconnects, or that customer will disconnect from you. I encourage you to lean into what motivates you. Become a real detective in pursuit of what makes you tick and learn to study people to better understand what makes them do what they do. This will prepare you to make incredible connections with your customers and all those who you encounter.

Getting the direct feedback on you, your Special Teams players, your CXO, and your Sales Team, will give both you and them the roadmap to accomplishing your goals.

These are all available at *chrisjenningsgroup.com*.

REFERRAL MADNESS AND TRACKING PROGRESS

It's late February 2023 as I write this. In a couple of weeks, my favorite sporting phenomenon starts: March Madness. Yes to the tournament, yes to the brackets, yes to the competition, the drive, the energy and the sheer enjoyment that many of us derive as we watch the results unfold!

While you may not make a turnaround three-pointer with no time on the clock, you do have several open shots, which I want you to take, like any coach would tell his or her shooters. Take the shot!

I believe you can do this, and I am hoping that by this point, you do too.

As noted earlier, one of the ways to improve your results is to make sure that you track it. One of my favorite tracking tools is the Referral Madness chart that you see below. If you add a new client due to your sales or marketing effort, their name gets added to the lefthand side of the bracket, thus starting a new potential chain of highly profitable referrals from the newly won customer.

What should happen over time is that, as you get more referrals from one client to the next, your referral pay off grows exponentially. Like I said, don't quit before the miracle happens. Don't judge your efforts on today's results, judge your efforts based on your follow-through with your commitments to yourself and others.

What should happen, as pictured next, is that you develop a huge following of clients, each coming from the one before them. As you will see, it will take less and less effort, the results will multiply, and you will win.

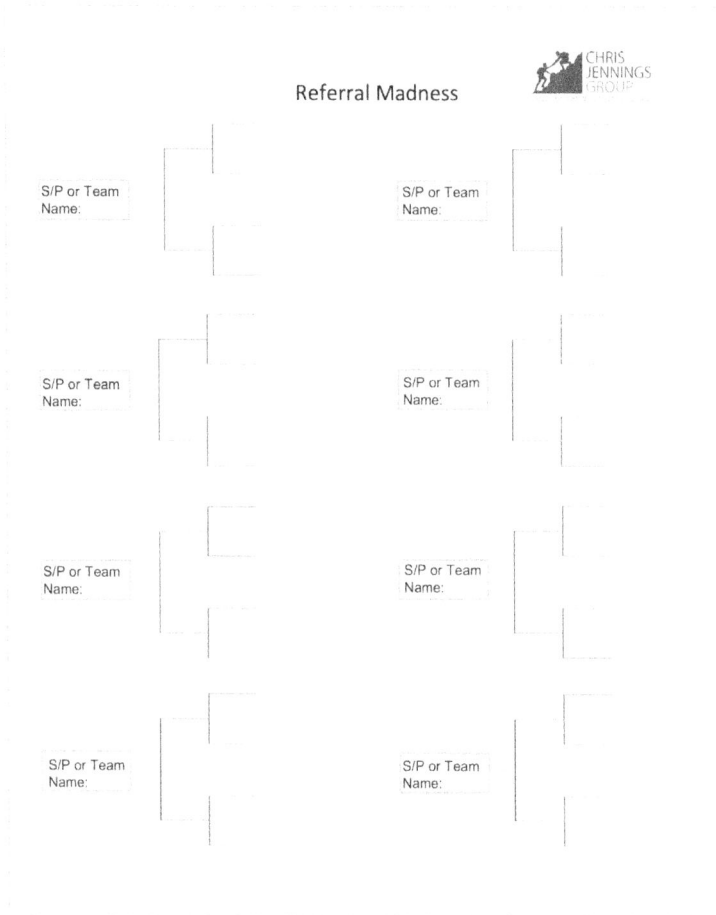

Referral Madness

CHRIS
JENNINGS
GROUP

S/P or Team
Name:

S/P or Team
Name:

S/P or Team
Name:

S/P or Team
Name:

S/P or Team
Name:

S/P or Team
Name:

S/P or Team
Name:

S/P or Team
Name:

Referral Madness — Chris Jennings Group

Let's say you enrolled in a coaching program with us, and asked us to look at your Referral Madness Bracket. If all we saw were single individual clients that you won through trade show exhibits, cold calls, and leads off your website...

What does that tell you?

It tells me that you—and probably your entire organization along with you—are working way too hard for too little return. I want you all to economize energy that regularly gets reinvested in your clients, your teammates, your family, and every community that energizes you.

The best way to do that is to engage your customers as an extension of your sales force. With or without compensation. Install all the systems covered here for you, and this will be a forgone conclusion.

COMPENSATION FOR CUSTOMERS AND YOUR TEAM

Personally, I don't know that you have to pay either group anything more than they would get normally by working with you. That being said, I do want to address a few questions that will naturally come up in your mind.

Compensating Customers

Previously I stated that the main reason I think your customers will want to refer you and keep working with you is that you do an amazing job, and you very thoughtfully put into practice the principles that I have shared with you in this book. Clearly, there will be many times when it seems like that isn't enough. With that in mind, here are a few quick ideas about rewarding your customers.

- Make it specific to the customer. If they love Vegas, then a sponsored conference/trip/invite may be appropriate. But if they hate Vegas, it works against you, not for you. A thoughtful gift at an unexpected time is preferred.

- Honor a group of clients at the end of the year with a really cool banquet. Maybe part informational, part pure entertainment. It could be you take your top 10 referring clients to a Lakers Game in a luxury box, and start the evening off with a speaker on a universally appealing subject. If you have a customer who hates that idea, maybe be ready with a day at the spa for the right individual, or limited edition of Wambats series of Books.

- Maybe there is a unique concierge level service with a select staff member dedicated to expediting orders for this group.

- Maybe special shipping terms.

All I would say is, not cash, not just a rebate, and maybe nothing at all. Use your discretion for what's appropriate. Many companies disallow this sort of reward anyways, so it may be a moot point.

Compensating Your People

My suggestion is always to install the process first, and then figure out if any compensation adjustment is warranted. Perhaps the team is happy just having better client relationships.

Perhaps the increase in profit naturally allows you to bonus the whole company based on shared results.

Perhaps you double down on the recognition company wide, at home, and in the community by celebrating certain successes.

All of these are possible.

My hope is that your profits dictate the right course of action, and that you regularly promote from within and the team feels incredibly appreciated, celebrated, and compensated in all ways possible. No one size fits all to give you—just my perspective, and experience.

You can also look at various compensation models on our website *chrisjenningsgroup.com*, and our first book, *Conversations Made Easy: Building Your Playbook for Connecting with Customers.*

CLOSING COMMENTS

Today, two different local teams won their games: the LA Lakers and UCLA Basketball. Both were comeback wins based on stellar defense. In each game, they used the fact they were behind to double down on their process and execute all the way to the final buzzers. Both games were clinched with less than ten seconds on the clock.

Your own margin of victory often looks a lot like those close games. And in the games you don't win, your lessons from the losses are all valuable. We're all learning every day. Don't quit before the miracle happens—especially since most of your competitors *will* quit! If you're the one who fights for every lesson and diligently works towards perfecting the process in your environment, I can promise you that the results will be plentiful for you, your team, and your customers.

Here's a quick recap of everything you learned in this book.

THE CLIENT RETENTION MATRIX

The model I laid out for you to follow guarantees increased profits with execution. So, while your competitors are settling for halfway there, you now have the keys to the kingdom.

Get your CXO busy overseeing the installation of the 10 Systems, build out the custom trail map for your team to follow, and notice the dollars hitting the bottom line and your team reveling in the sense of pride from a job well done.

BeUSEFUL: EXTERNAL CUSTOMERS

This is your model for great conversations with clients—for the people who *don't* like to talk to clients. Save time, get more done, and work toward hitting the maximum lifetime potential value of every client.

BeUSEFUL: INTERNAL CUSTOMERS

Use that same model for great conversations with coworkers. Get the team on the same page, reduce turnover, and increase engagement by the results that come from true mutual understanding.

ONBOARDING NEW CLIENTS AND PROJECTS

This model sets you and your client up for success, and initiates the process for turning customers into raving fans and all-star clients.

WHAT'S YOUR STORY?

Understand your internal story so that you can build the confidence in yourself to take your career on a journey to new places—doing

new things that build even more confidence, and leaving the old stories and baggage behind.

GETTING GREAT AT REFERRALS

Find new opportunities through existing connections, with low-
to-no cost of sales, and very little time invested.

SPECIAL TEAMS

This model gets your entire organization to work together, making
sales and servicing customers a team sport through a highly coordinated effort.

INDIVIDUAL PERFORMER TOOLKIT

The Individual Performer Toolkit is filled with shortcuts, trail maps,
and smart ideas about how to make asking for referrals even easier.

LEADERSHIP TOOLKIT

This contains best practices to becoming the leader you always
wanted—everything you need to hit your true potential.

DO GREAT WORK

Recently, a friend was telling me and some other friends a story about
something that happened at her work. She works for a larger services
based company that is thought of as one of the best companies in the
world—any vendor would consider themselves very fortunate to be
working with her company.

My friend was leading a portion of a project to integrate a new CRM into their organization, and the story she shared centered around a disgruntled team member of their vendor's company. She is an important Special Teams member of this CRM provider and clearly there was a breakdown in internal communication at the CRM vendor, which resulted in them becoming a bad partner, not connecting with my friend and her team at all.

To make it more difficult, this implementation team was held offshore. In and of itself, this isn't a bad thing at all. The problem started with the vendor having a bad internal handoff, then continued with poor onboarding and a disconnect to not fully understanding the customer's Org Chart.

My friend and her team were given the runaround, causing over a month's delay in the install, and rather than own the problem, that implementation team threw it back on my friend's team, giving them a bunch of attitude in the process.

I would call that a *huge fumble*. If they had a CXO, and if they had communicated more clearly in an attempt to truly **BeUseful**, odds are that this could have been avoided.

I hope you haven't gotten the sense that I live in some Shangri-la fantasy world where I don't think any problems exist. I don't mind problems. In fact, I kind of like them, in that they give you a chance to get better.

My issue is more: why create problems that don't need to be created? Why not focus a little more energy in the process, and help everybody in your organization get through their day with fewer headaches and less grief?

Life is short. People take pride in doing great work. If you as a leader have made it easier for your people to succeed, they will be your biggest fans—creating fans of your team, and opening doors for all concerned.

If you can execute the **Client Retention Matrix** close to how I laid it out for you in this read, I encourage you to post your results on our website. Maybe ask to get interviewed for our podcast or You Tube channel. Not for the glory, but to pay it forward!

Help the next person in line learn from your experience. Shine a light on what is possible and see what it feels like to have an impact on the world around you.

The other day as I was driving to an early meeting, I called up my wife Lenna, who was also driving to work. "We both get to go to work today and help some other people have better lives," I said. "We get to use our God-given skills for the purpose of helping people in their jobs, at their homes, and in their communities."

So, for us, we've stopped working for a paycheck, and started working for a purpose. I wouldn't call this a career; to us now, it's more of a calling.

We let go of what we get out of going to work and focus our attention on what we give by going to work. We're humble servants hoping to make a real difference, realizing that it's not always obvious in the hustle and bustle of the day-to-day grind—but it is there, if we look for it.

I hope this book has given you the tools you've been looking for, and that you teach these tools to others that would be drawn into a servant mindset. I encourage you to elevate your purpose each day to the good you bring to the workplace and the other communities that you serve and the families you live with, and take great joy in your efforts and your learnings every day.

Ask for help for the tough parts. So many resources are available on our website at *chrisjenningsgroup.com.* Use them, learn from them, and teach them to others.

I hope you have enjoyed our time together! Stay tuned for my next and final book, where I take everything I have ever learned and apply it purely to the lives that matter most: yours, your loved ones, and those in all your communities.

It's going to be fun, it's going to be different, and it's going to make every conversation easier. I promise.

Humbly yours,

Chris T. Jennings

ABOUT THE AUTHOR

Chris Jennings is the owner of Chris Jennings Group, a sales, leadership, and business development consultancy. For nearly three decades, Chris has worked with thousands of businesses to help improve communication with customers and form stronger connections. He is a top-rated speaker for Vistage International and has coached thousands of private and industry-specific organizations. A former triathlete, Chris is the proud father of three adult daughters. He and his wife Lenna live in Orange County, California.

www.ingramcontent.com/pod-product-compliance
Lightning Source LLC
Chambersburg PA
CBHW030457210326

41597CB00013B/709